John Lloyd is editor of the *Financial Times Magazine*, and a regular contributor to *Prospect* and other journals. He has won four national awards for his reporting. His previous books include *Loss Without Limit: The British Miners' Strike* (1986) and *Rebirth of a Nation: An Anatomy of Russia* (1998).

By the same author

Loss Without Limit: The British Miners' Strike

Rebirth of a Nation: An Anatomy of Russia

What the Media
Are Doing to Our Politics

JOHN LLOYD

CONSTABLE • LONDON

Constable & Robinson Ltd
3 The Lanchesters
162 Fulham Palace Road
London W6 9ER
www.constablerobinson.com

First published in the UK by Constable,
an imprint of Constable & Robinson Ltd 2004

A copy of the British Library Cataloguing in Publication data
is available from the British Library

ISBN 1–84119–900–1

Printed and bound in the EU

2 4 6 8 10 9 7 5 3 1

Contents

Acknowledgements

Grateful thanks to Barry Cox, Anthony Giddens and Graham Watts for reading an early draft of this essay and offering critical and detailed advice on changes. There are too many conversations and insights given to me by public figures, private individuals and fellow journalists to list all to whom thanks are due. I would mention only John Birt, Ralph Dahrendorf, Chrystia Freeland, David Goodhart, Ian Hargreaves, Jean Seaton, Yuri Senokosov and three successive editors of the *Financial Times* – Geoffrey Owen, Richard Lambert and Andrew Gowers.

Thanks too, to Claudia Dyer, Dan Hind and Pam Dix at Constable & Robinson Ltd.

Introduction

I N THE time that has passed since an early morning BBC
broadcast in May 2003 reported that the Government had
deliberately falsified a key reason for going to war in Iraq, reflection within and about the media has deepened and widened. In
broadcasting, a new urgency has been felt in the debate – which
had been already under way: is, indeed, permanent – on the
provision of its 'public service' component. A new questioning
has appeared, though sporadic, on the ability of the press to report
on public affairs. Many voices had been raised in recent years,
arguing that the British media were destructive – perhaps uniquely
destructive – of public communication and of democratic practise.
After the May 2003 broadcast and its consequences, there has been
some sign that arguments for a renewal of the values and tasks of
free media were being attended to more closely, and that a real
debate on what media do to our politics and civil society might
begin.

This essay is an attempt to argue for that renewal. It is an
argument for intervention in the media to secure better outcomes
for readers and viewers than the media would achieve left to their
own, competitive devices. Some of these interventions, in broadcasting, can only be undertaken by the state. Others, in both the
press and broadcasting, should only be undertaken by the media
themselves, together with other forces in civil society – and these

1

are the most important. Regulation can achieve only a framework: the culture of free media can only be created, and renewed, by those who work in them and those who are concerned with their workings.

The state should get into this area as a *legislator* as little as possible – and when it does, it should be for a clear public purpose, of safeguarding democratic argument and the provision of information when the market fails in these tasks. But government and politicians should be in the *debate*, more than they have been, since they represent the people whose freedoms the media claim they are in business to protect. The key element, however, is civil society – the networks of public policy actors, public opinion, independent political and campaigning activities, market provisions, institutional rivalries and the media themselves – which must determine how our society reflects itself to itself.

In a phrase, this essay proposes a social market in media. Britain has a huge advantage over other states in sustaining such an outcome: it has the BBC, the most prestigious and best-funded public broadcaster in the world. Government will inevitably have something to say and do about its governance and its editorial framework, as it will about those of independent broadcasters. But socially valuable outcomes in both broadcasting and the media can only be achieved consistently by a belief in their value on the part of the media themselves – that is, the people whose job it is to represent the world to their fellow citizens.

Given that the broadcast of 29 May 2003 has been so important to this and all other narratives on the British media since it happened, it's as well to remind ourselves what it consisted of. Here is a transcript, as broadcast on the 'Today' programme, at 06.07.

John Humphrys ('Today' programme presenter): The government is facing more questions this morning over its claims about weapons of mass destruction (WMD). Our defence correspondent is Andrew Gilligan. This in particular, Andy, is Tony Blair saying, they'd [Iraqi missiles] be ready to go within 45 minutes?

Andrew Gilligan ('Today' programme defence correspondent): That's right, that was the central claim in his dossier which he published in September, the main case if you like against Iraq, and the main statement of the government's belief of what it thought Iraq was up to and what we've been told by one of the senior officials in charge of drawing up that dossier was that, actually, the government probably knew that that 45-minute figure was wrong, even before it decided to put it in. What this person says, it was actually a rather bland production. It didn't, the draft prepared for Mr Blair by the intelligence agencies, actually didn't say very much more than was public knowledge already and Downing Street, our source says, ordered a week before publication, ordered it to be sexed up, to be made more exciting and ordered more facts to be, to be discovered.

JH: When you say 'more facts to be discovered' does that suggest they may not have been facts?

AG: Well, our source says that the dossier, as it was finally published, made the intelligence services unhappy because, to quote the source, he said there was basically, that there was, there was, there was unhappiness because it didn't reflect the considered view they were putting forward, that's a quote from our source, and essentially the 45-minute point was, was probably the most important thing that was added. And the reason it hadn't been put in the original draft was that it was, it was only, it only came from one source and most of the other claims were from two, and the intelligence agencies say they don't really believe it was necessarily true because they thought the person making the claim had actually made a mistake, it got, it had got mixed up.

3

JH: Does any of this matter now, all this, all these months later? The war's been fought and won.

AG: Well, the 45 minutes isn't just a detail, it did go to the heart of the government's case that Saddam was an imminent threat and it was repeated four times in the dossier, including by the Prime Minister himself, in the foreword: so I think it probably does matter. Clearly, you know, if, if it, if it was, if it was wrong, things do, things are, got wrong in good faith, but if they knew it was wrong before they actually made the claim, that's perhaps a bit more serious.

JH: Andrew, many thanks; more about that later.

Never, in his long career, had John Humphrys done a better sign-off than that.

The broadcast, government's protests against it and the controversy it generated, claimed the life of its main source – Dr David Kelly, a government weapons expert. It was the main object of inquiries and reports by two parliamentary select committees, those on intelligence and on foreign affairs. And it was the prompt for the Hutton Inquiry and subsequent report – which put into the public arena more information and analysis of the secret services and their relationship with government than had ever been revealed so soon after the event at any time before. Indeed – and this isn't the subject of this essay – the effect on the intelligence world may in the long term be larger, for itself and for society, than on that of the media.

Andrew Gilligan's report has become a central fact in the battles about the media and their relationship with power. It was not necessary that it do so. It could have been a minor matter. At more or less any period in the three months after it had been aired, the fury it caused within government could have been defused by an apology from the BBC that it was inaccurate, as it was quickly realized, by at least some editors at the BBC, that it was. But because it was defended and opposed with equal vigour, it thus had to play a part which still continues: as a symbol used in sharply opposing ways.

For many in the media and outside them, the two-way report became and remains a talisman of media freedom: the testimony of a brave and properly sceptical reporter who shone a beam of light into a murky area and told the country what was being distorted in its name. In this version, the slips and mistakes were secondary, even – as in the mis-naming of David Kelly as an intelligence source – necessary. The key, in this version of events, is that a vital truth came out. The document was 'sexed up'. Exactly how and by whom, one could leave to the historians.

This reaction is at the heart of the journalists' dilemma – which is also a dilemma for the rest of society, whether it is conscious of it or not. That is, that much of what occurs, especially in times of crisis, does so behind closed doors – yet what happens there is vitally important to the citizen. Getting information on the many tightly knotted strings of information, which uncoil themselves behind closed doors, is a fraught business. Information from sources is likely to be partial, self-interested for one reason or the other on the part of the source and often at the service of a point other than accuracy. That is, the source has his or her own case to make and is using the media to do it. Sometimes, the more willing a source is to give information, the less reliable it is. The more vital any closed-door process, the more the insiders are enjoined to secrecy: indeed, it may be a sacking offence, or even a crime, to give information to a journalist.

The journalist seeking such information is asking insiders to break the trust placed in them by giving details of events supposed to be confidential. The source may do it cynically or opportunistically. If these motives are absent, the only moral framework to which the journalist can appeal when asking for details is a larger one than the trust placed in the insider by the employer or the state (which might be the same thing). That larger ethic is some version of the public's right to know – the ethic that has sustained journalism's claim to be a central part of the democratic process for the four centuries of its existence, and which sustains it still. For many in and out of the media, both Andrew Gilligan and his source, David Kelly, were acting within the protection of this ethic, larger than the duty the latter owed to the government which employed him. The ethic was larger than the breach of confidence, larger than the mistakes.

For others, the report, for all its brevity (partly *because* of its brevity), displays many of the features which are most prominent and troubling in the way in which news is defined, reported and analysed in Britain – and, in different ways, elsewhere.

First, it was carelessly done. Introduced in a way which assumed prior knowledge to make the report comprehensible, it contained a series of statements which are difficult to defend. Within the first few sentences, for example, the statements that the government claim that Iraqi missiles could be readied within 45 minutes were 'the central claim' and 'the main case, if you like, against Iraq' are both wrong – in the second case, wildly so. The main case against Iraq was never that it had missiles ready to fire within 45 minutes. However, its main virtue and its main selling point, within most media organizations at the time it was made, was that it was highly critical of the government. It could not, in fact, be much more so – since it accuses the government of lying. More, the introduction by Humphrys makes it clear that the prime minister himself ('Tony Blair [is] saying they'd be ready to go within 45 minutes') is doing the lying. It thus gained traction by fitting into an existing narrative: that the government had taken the country into the war on false grounds. Indeed, as I'll argue, that was fitted within an even larger narrative – that the government was not to be trusted on anything. Its contribution to this overall narrative seems likely to have been enough to have secured its place in the bulletin, even in the shambolic form it took – and to be repeated throughout the day, albeit in a slightly diluted form.

Second, it was a grave charge, but it was lightly made. The substance of the report could be amply defended as being in the public interest: there are few more urgent things for citizens to know than that an elected government is systematically lying to them. At the same time, the seriousness of the charge increases the responsibility on the reporters and editors to be sure of the facts. But the editors didn't know it was well founded: they didn't check that it was before it was broadcast, and quite soon after it went out, they discovered it wasn't. Indeed, it was implicitly acknowledged that the 'hard' Gilligan version – 'the government probably knew that that 45-minute figure was wrong' – was dropped, in favour of a vaguer claim that it had 'sexed up' the dossier – which means more or less the same thing, especially since the first, hard version had not been corrected. Humphrys' question – 'does all this really matter?' – indicates that he simply assumed government mendacity, assumed a cynical universe and was prepared to discuss the aftermath. Having accused the government of lying, the BBC took the posture – in the same broadcast – of one prepared to be surprised at the fuss. Government lies of that magnitude call for media mobilization of equal magnitude. It didn't get anything like it.

Third, the BBC response to challenge was ignorant defiance – and remained so, even after the publication of the Hutton Report. The BBC, having refused to face up to the implications of the report, also refused to admit it was wrong. Greg Dyke resigned still protesting that it was 'basically correct'. A large part of its own justification was that the prime minister's director of communications, Alastair Campbell, had complained so much that a fresh complaint against Gilligan was hardly worth taking seriously or investigating (famously, Dyke, the editor-in-chief, did not read the brief transcript for three weeks after it was broadcast). The attitude to the government was – 'they would say that, wouldn't they?' The phrase is that of Mandy Rice-Davies (as quoted, 'he would, wouldn't he?'), a player in the Profumo scandal which engulfed the Conservative government in the late 1950s/early 1960s, uttered almost exactly 40 years before, at the dawning of the new age of journalism. This new age broke with the old in increasingly systematically disbelieving authorities' explanations – especially that of government.

In 2003, the posture of much of the media was that politics was a degraded profession. It was common currency everywhere, as we'll see – from tabloid to broadsheet, fact to fiction. That story – a master story, the story which framed others which dealt in the detail – had been written, progressively strongly, for decades. So strong was this master story that facts which ran contrary to it could not be accepted. So strong was it that the BBC, the oldest and most admired public service broadcaster in the world, was able to justify to its critics and to itself a report of huge significance, which broke most of the proclaimed rules of journalistic inquiry.

The report into the Kelly affair was greeted by much of the media with fury. Lord Hutton's report, with its largely unequivocal backing for the government's side of the affair as revealed through the many hours of testimony to the inquiry he chaired, had to be rejected by many commentators and editors on the same grounds: it simply did not fit into the narrative which they had invested so much time, energy – and marketing strategy – in constructing. The BBC had recovered itself enough to do a careful account of the affair in a 'Panorama' – aired, exceptionally, in prime time – and covered the report itself fairly. Much of the rest of the media saw it as a 'WHITEWASH' – in the word used by the *Independent* the day after its publication, covering all of its front page. That is, it was assumed that the stench of the government's corruption had been drenched in perfume by a compliant, or at best stupid, judge. In the drive for a master narrative of political rottenness, those in the media most active in promoting it had to degrade all other institutions – including the judiciary – which were not compliant with its will. (The *Independent* won Newspaper of the Year in the British Press Awards in March 2004.)

The Kelly affair and the Hutton Report revealed a profession – and a public – split between seeing in the original Gilligan report a pioneering piece of journalism, even if flawed, and those who saw it as a piece of journalism whose flaws were too great to qualify it as anything other than a serious mistake which should have been rectified as much and as soon as possible. Since it was not put right, it went on to become a cause celebre: and to act as the starting point for a reflection on the media and their responsibilities. That is how it's treated here.

The media, in the twenty-first century, are in Britain at the height of their powers – a position shared by their counterparts in no other country, even the US. The population watches, on average, 28 hours of television a week, and listens to 24 hours of radio a day; in 2003, nearly 35 million people read a daily or Sunday newspaper, 36.5 million read a magazine and nearly 25 million people accessed the Internet. The reading component of that is declining, if slowly, but the total time spent with the media far exceeds that spent on any other activity and, for many, that spent on all other activities combined, except work.

Nothing – not religious belief, not political debate and argument, not even conversation with friends and family – possesses the command over mass attention that the media have taken as their own. Their themes dominate public and private lives. Their definitions of what is right or wrong, true or false, impose them-selves on politics and on the public domain. Their narratives construct the world we don't immediately experience – which, for nearly all of us, is most of the world. Democratic rule has the sanction of the vote: but media power has the sanction of audience. The first has been tending to decline, in some cases to alarmingly low levels – down to around 20 per cent in local and European elections, not much above 50 per cent in general elections. The second is largely growing, as the media add more and more entertaining products, services and choice for consumers who are increasingly placed in the position of indulged children: spoilt for choice.

Political power in a democracy cannot sustain itself without engagement and debate, on the part of the public as well as of the political classes and it cannot work without demanding a good deal of citizens, most obviously demanding large amounts of their money in the form of taxes. The media demand little apart from purchase – at relatively low prices – and attention at an intensity of the viewer's choosing: anything from excitement to snoozing will do.

After the Hutton Report was published, newspapers carried out polls on which institution, government or BBC, retained more public trust. However the question was posed, the BBC always won. That is, the most powerful media institution in the country, which labours ceaselessly and often successfully to entertain its audience, won in a contest with a second-term government, which had just demanded that the country go to war. Not a matter for much surprise.

Journalism in Britain – in Britain above all other democratic states – had been assailed by a series of assumptions and attitudes, which created the 'accident waiting to happen' that was Andrew Gilligan's broadcast. The accident was waiting to happen because the media had become increasingly destructive of their environment, increasingly prone to the 'cynical assumption that politicians are born liars and rogues'. Their environment is the institutions, practises and traditions of the democratic state; their rights and privileges derive from these – their power would be nothing without them. Indeed, they would have no power, but would be reduced to the slave media which we know from authoritarian states, where political power drives out all others. Or rather, it uses the form of independence while making the content its own – as authoritarian states make the media an extension of their rulers' power.

Or again – as we shall see from the contrast with contemporary Italy – media become so heavily politicized and so leached of independent news judgement that no one can tell how far they are giving an account of the truth, or are being prevented from doing so, or are reacting to a false charge with false, or overdrawn, charges of their own. Media create an environment of understanding: if they don't have a large space for rational discussion, careful reporting, wide contextualization, then we are left with the trading of charges, insults and opinions. These are necessary, or at any rate inevitable, in a democracy: but they don't get at the truth in themselves.

In the last two decades, the understanding that media depend on democratic institutions which work well has been damaged. The public sphere has not been seen as one to preserve, but as an area on which tournaments may be staged on the one hand, and on the other as a landscape dotted with forests, in whose depths reporters can hunt for prey, dragging them out into the light of day on the end of their spears.

This essay is largely about the news media, but the news media have rarely been, and certainly are not now, separable from other forms of media and other forms of power. It is also largely about the UK, but the trends described in it are worldwide, even if media

11

retain a distinctive national stamp – the more so, since they are among the most important carriers of the national language, in written and spoken forms.

They have always been suborned to political purposes; have always operated part in, part outside, the world of entertainment; have always expressed, directly or indirectly, the interests of their owners. Part of their drama has always been a striving for independence from the powers that own or control or seek to master them. This drama is the one most constantly celebrated by the media and their most powerful actors: the drama of men and women striving to be free to tell the truth. In this drama, the villains are (in a muted and often private way) the owners, more often officials and, above all, politicians.

The struggle between politicians and the media is critical because this conflict, which has usually been represented as a healthy clash of independent institutions in a democratic policy, has for some time assumed the character of a zero-sum-game struggle for power. It is part of the aim here to show that this is not necessarily healthy, because it diminishes, rather than aerates or increases, freedom, and it increases the anomie and distrust within civil society. This is an argument which many in the media dislike, for it strikes at the heart both of their idealistic self-belief and their everyday practises and use of their power. But it should be made, and should be made from within the media themselves; indeed, if it is to work and to renew the media culture, it is ultimately the only place from which it *can* be made.

Politicians and media people do not appear, always, to struggle. There is huge collusion between them; indeed New Labour built its election and its governance strategy, in very large part, on a more intensive engagement and collusion with the media than any party/government had before. That makes it an unlikely object of sympathy for its treatment at the media's hand – and in most media stories about the government, it certainly isn't. This is wrong: this government, as well as others, are victims at the hands of the media, even if they have connived at their own victimhood. But important as it is to understand how and why politicians in particular and public figures in general are victimized, it is less important than the threat the media now pose to democratic institutions. It is this threat, ironically at its greatest when the media are apparently at their most fearless, which is the main line of argument in this book.

The conflict between politics and the media is generally supposed, certainly by the media, to be unequal: in the end, politics can always trump the media because it has the power – state power – to do so. Politicians can pass laws restricting the media. They can refuse to give access to journalists, limit what they are told and see and even arrest them. But in practise, state power in this regard is relatively weak. Access has tended to broaden; what is seen and told has tended to increase; the extremes of banning and arrest become all but impossible. This will continue to be the tendency, while liberal democracies remain what they are (if, of course, they cease to remain so, then all bets are off, including, and perhaps more seriously, for liberal politicians of the right and left).

In liberal democratic *practise*, the battle is unequal the other way round. Politics and politicians depend on the media for access to people. If the media do not allow that access, then politicians have few other ways of making known their priorities, programmes and proposals. The public meeting and walkabout continue to be part of a campaign; but for the leaders and principal personalities of parties, the campaigns are made for the media. This is, of course, a political 'choice'; and politicians have chosen to be extraordinarily accommodating to the media – so much so that the media can with justice point to politicians as collaborating with them in producing a new kind of media-friendly politician, who has in turn become an object of media scorn. But the fact that politicians collaborate in the degradation of politics is not an argument for degradation.

That access to the media which is granted to politicians is on increasingly harsh terms. We have become accustomed to interviews with politicians and other public figures being constructed round the interviewees' most neuralgic points: we don't, in the main, expect a discussion in the round about the field of problems in which the public figure has to operate. And since public figures in politics, business and other institutions have both come to expect this approach and wish to pursue their objectives by talking up their plans and achievements, they have acquired shields. These come in the shape of media training designed to make them bland, or guarded, or able to change the subject, and/or in the person of media handlers, who seek to minimize damage and choice. Both sides assume bad faith: the interviewer assumes evasion, at worst deceit; the interviewee assumes concentration on sore points, at worst a fight from which the interviewer would normally emerge the winner. The irony here is increasingly obvious: a technique to elicit information and increase clarity produces the smoke of battle and the fog of war.

Many of the major presenters of TV current affairs, as many in the press, see politicians as a debased class. Usually this is expressed in an attitude and a tone, in a concentration on an area in which a public figure is constrained to be ambiguous, or discreet, or silent. Sometimes, as we'll see, they make these views explicit, seeing politicians in particular as a class fallen far short both of past performance and present ideals. Since they are the most powerful, prominent and most highly rewarded of their profession, editorial control over the major presenters is light and emulation of them by reporters and presenters further down the hierarchy is encouraged. How could they fail to be taken as role models, in a world where role models are increasingly created, rather than being lodged in the traditions of institutions or the sanctity of religions?

The common drive of the media is to expose and to embarrass. Owners rarely, and most editors even more rarely, act as agents of social responsibility – that is, putting the case that this story or that broadcast would be damaging to society, or to an individual. Increasingly, such a case would attract ridicule – from all sides, especially if it was made about the government. To the contemporary British newsroom, the objections credited to the *Washington Post* editor – Ben Bradlee during the unfolding case against President Richard Nixon which became known as Watergate – that here was a story which impugned the highest officials in the land and thus had to be treated with the greatest of care – do not, generally, operate. What does operate is what Katharine Graham, president of the *Washington Post* company, in her memoir, warned against – that of succumbing to 'the romantic tendency [for the press] to picture itself in the role of a heroic and beleaguered champion, defending all virtues against overwhelming odds'.

The media have an unwritten rule not to divulge their power. They are critically important players in public life: account for huge amounts of leisure time; give news round the clock on each day of the year; stage the dramas and spectacles which provide the content for much of the common interests of acquaintances and friends; teach attitudes; introduce trends; show how to display emotions. They have gone from being enfolded in, or even marginalized by, the more powerful institutions of the state and the set patterns of communal and private life, to enfolding them. They have made the world their oyster: or rather, they *are* the oyster, em-pearling their audience with their glow of ceaseless interest, ceaseless novelty, ceaseless sensation.

They make and re-make the versions of the world with which we live – and yet when the news media represent the world, they largely excuse themselves from it. Contemporary life is inexplicable without an account of the part the media play in it, yet media studies are put in a specialist area of the academy, originally a sub-branch of sociology or social anthropology, now an increasingly popular subject from GCSE level up – but not one in which the media's power, and ability to interpret the world, is much discussed. Politicians who question the power of the media are dismissed as shifting the blame from their own mistakes: politicians who court the media are caricatured as lackeys, as if they had no overpowering incentive to seek to ensure that their message would travel, relatively undamaged, down some channels.

The division between news and comment has tended to erode and the habit of comment has become general. In part this is because the number of columnists has increased many-fold. The late Hugo Young, in the introduction to a collection of his columns published after his death in September 2003, wrote that in the 1950s there were no political columnists. In the early 2000s, Young had encountered an acquaintance who had been asked by the prime minister's office to compile a list 'of all national newspaper columnists to whom Downing Street might want to get a political message across. His survey wasn't yet complete but so far he had counted no fewer than 221 of them.' The comment demonstrates the evident fact that comment is now the habit of our age; it also points to the concomitant trend, which is that the line between the fact and the comment is now gone. The reporter and the presenter are much freer to suggest, or even impose, their own explicit or implicit judgement on the process described than at any time since the broadcast media became dominant.

In newspapers, the tendency has resulted in the privileging of reportage which is suffused with moral or other judgements – as the reporting of some dailies, notably the *Independent* and the *Daily Mirror*, of the Iraq war. In broadcasting, no such overtly

16

biased 'comm-portage' is possible. Yet in the hands of the most skilful broadcasters, judgements are made which are not of a right/left political bias; rather, they are descriptions of the lowly, degraded state of public life – by implication. When in the spring of 2003, the Labour politician Estelle Morris came under strong pressure and finally resigned, the BBC's political editor Andrew Marr said of her in a TV news broadcast that 'she's dead meat'. It was a phrase inconceivable to an earlier generation of broadcasters, injecting the image of the slaughter house into the political process.

This – and countless other such displays – are evidence of a knowledge of power. Politics dominated the media until some time around the 1960s, the time when hard questioning in interviews, investigative reporting and TV satire of politics began. Since then, politics and politicians have been – often literally – on the defensive, constantly ceding ground to the media in what the latter can ask and how they can ask it, what they can and should know and in their willingness to take part in the harsh or derisive representations of the political process which the media stage under the name of current affairs. There were many gains for civil society in that process; many of these are in the opening of previously needlessly secret places. But the story is not all one of triumph – even if media people celebrate the end of politics' supremacy over them as the advent of 'real' journalism, especially in broadcast news and current affairs. They see the vast shift as a time when we passed from a journalism whose reporters asked questions of the kind: 'Have you anything you wish to say to us, Prime Minister?' to the reported injunction of Harry Evans, editor of the *Sunday Times* from 1967 to 1981: 'Always ask yourself, when you interview a politician – why is this bastard lying to me?' It was indeed the advent of a questioning, revealing and stone-turning approach to news, but it inevitably carried another side. In adopting the tropes of investigation, journalists made themselves the arbiters of public life and public persons, and claimed to be the main guardians of truth and morality. It is that other side which has become, in turn, dominant: and it is that other side, which can be a dark one, which needs to be examined now for its effect on politics and society.

This *is* a struggle for power. The media strive to have power over the same people and for the same reasons as do politicians. We need people to follow us – that is, buy our papers or watch or listen to our programmes. More, we need them to believe our stories, our versions of the world – or if not believe them (for people would go mad if they tried seriously to believe, and thus act on, all or even some of the stories spun to them every day by the industrious media) then at least be diverted enough by them to form a habit of buying or switching on, day after day, filling more and more hours with the fantasies we weave for them.

Politicians also tell stories – they tell stories in order to be elected; and once elected, they tell stories about the nature of the challenges and the kind of measures and reforms necessary to meet these challenges. These stories can be more or less close to reality, but at least reality follows them: that is, they can be judged by reference to real consequences and further real consequences follow in terms of votes. Our stories usually do not have serious consequences – at least, not to us. In that sense, the Kelly affair was an exception: the government protested, forced an issue and – largely because the BBC refused to admit any kind of mistake – the issue went to an inquiry and a report. This led to changes in the BBC and should lead to further shifts in the way in which the media are perceived and – hopefully – act.

In achieving power, the media had to create their galaxy of celebrities – the news media doing so later than entertainment, but ultimately as efficiently and with a much greater aura of moral worth. But fame in journalism has a logic which is impossible to buck. To become a news celebrity means leaving the business of doing news as a reporter – that is, looking for something which approximates to a truth – and using the pursuit of news as a conduit to celebrity. The belief which most prominent news journalists have in the moral goodness of their profession must become solidified into a dogma, or into an attitude, or both. Thus the stars are obliged to go through routines which demonstrate the essence which has made them celebrities – much as a star will always be asked to sing the old favourite.

The majority of journalists never reach celebrity status and many feel resentful and upset by this. Such resentment was a prime mover in the publication, in 2002, of *Bias*, a bilious book in which Bernard Goldberg, a former CBS reporter, alleged consistent liberal bias by the super-paid news anchormen of the three main US TV channels. The resentment is increased by a feeling that the non-celebrities have nothing to put in the place of stardom – no professional ethic, or satisfaction in doing good and necessary work. But, as I argue in the last part of this essay, there *is* something better to put in its place: journalism which is both detailed and subtle, which admits – indeed insists on – diversity in the causes of events and contradictory impulses in the leading characters who make events happen.

The process of the weakening of institutions and the growth in the importance of individualism has produced many and obvious benefits, above all, much greater care taken by officialdom and corporations of individual lives, preferences and rights. Among the downsides has been the cult of celebrity. In journalism, this has tended to emphasize the unpleasant side of the profession, always present – the tendency to intrusive and judgemental voyeurism. The desire for fame via the exposure of scandal has, with the inhibiting presence of once-powerful institutions withdrawn, been

19

given an open field on which to work. The strength of institutions – family, Church, authorities of various kinds, military, unions, corporations and above all the state – kept the journalists' cynical view of life in the background. Journalists had, at least for some of the time, to reflect and reproduce the rationales and propaganda of the institutions themselves; indeed, to do other was to risk professional suicide. But now, the decline in stature and above all in retributory power of the institutions, and the growth of kudos and monetary rewards from exposing, criticizing or merely creating a scandal around institutions and public figures, is so great that journalists are foolish if they do not use their personality – especially if it is a powerful one – to express itself in moral disapproval, contempt, mockery, intrusion and hectoring. The payback from doing so is fame and money; the blowback from those against whom one launches oneself is generally to be discounted. The greatest danger for the journalists who work at the sharp end of exposure is not making enough of a splash, and thus being seen as one who cannot deliver on scandal or revelation.

It is also part of the argument here that in despising politicians and in drastically reducing the space given to democratic debate, the media have made their worst mistake. The Gilligan broadcast was a small tip of one iceberg: it was supported by a much larger series of assumptions and confusions. Journalists confuse being subservient to politicians (which no free media can allow themselves to be) with being subservient to democratic politics. The media have not come up with a better idea than democratic politics, and they do not officially claim to have done so: but in many ways, explicitly and implicitly, they act as if they have. The media have claimed the right to judge and to condemn; more, they have decided – without being clear about the decision – that politics is a dirty game, played by devious people who tell an essentially false narrative about the world and thus deceive the British people.

20

This has not been the only, but it has been the increasingly dominant, narrative which the media have constructed about politics over the past decade or so and, though it has suffered some knocks, it remains dominant.

But it also remains in a kind of twilight world. It cannot exactly speak its name. The news media deal with serious issues every day, and their practitioners know enough to be aware that if the implicit charge of systematic mendacity were to be pressed, it would have to be proven. Gilligan's broadcast stepped over a line which the media have generally been careful not to cross. Normally, such overt accusations on such flimsy ground are eschewed for two reasons. First, there is the residual respect for journalistic procedure, absent in the case of the May 2003 BBC broadcast, which warns that most such accusations would fail the test of proof. Second and much more important, such accusations are not attempted because such an effort would defeat the object of the game. The object of the game is to leave a miasma of bad faith hanging about politics – never wholly said, and thus never in the realm where it must be convincingly denied. In this foggy struggle, the Kelly case cut through like a sudden shaft of light. A specific charge of lying (ultimately by the prime minister) was made and, unusually, was strongly challenged. And because the issues were rehearsed at such length in the Hutton Inquiry afterwards, it has become a rare and hugely significant piece of evidence in the relationship between the media and the political world – for Britain, of course, but by analogy many other political worlds, too.

There is a course for the media other than the one they have increasingly decisively chosen. It is to take their own protestations seriously. The news media's general claim when presenting a responsible face to the world is that they inform people about what they need to know to be active citizens, even if this claim is daily subservient to other goals such as entertaining, making a profit and increasing the prestige of journalists. But the goal of developing informed citizens need not be served by acts of constant aggression or attitudes of constant suspicion towards politicians and public officials. It could also be served – and better served – by understanding and taking seriously official and representatives' stated aims, indeed, by seeking an understanding of the public world which is richer than that attempted by most media organizations now. It is this approach that I'll try to argue for in the last part of this essay.

Michael Schudson, among the sharpest of the US media commentators, puts the matter this way:

> The well informed citizen is defined not by a consumer's familiarity with the contemporary catalogue of available information, but by a citizen's formed set of interests that make using the catalogue something more than a random effort. The news media increasingly help to provide the materials for the informational citizen, but they do not and cannot create the informed citizen.

Schudson is right that the media cannot create the informed citizen – but wrong if he suggests here that they cannot assist in creating such a figure. The civicness of citizens is now partly a product of the media. Robert Putnam, in *Bowling Alone*, saw entertainment television as the major factor in causing the breakdown of associations and of sociable, even family, activities, and lamented the decline in viewing news and current affairs programmes on television, especially when done in company. But what if the news increasingly partakes of entertainment – either because its content is the entertainment industry and personalities, or because it is presented in a way which plays to a pre-set morality play – or soap-opera – of good and evil? What if it does not, or cannot, in

Schudson's words, 'provide the materials for . . . the informed citizen'?

The search for a renewed civil society in which people are more civic – more fully engaged, better informed, less prey to crime and anti-social behaviour, more willing to volunteer, debate and vote – now consumes much space. It is an assumption common to intellectuals and commentators of the right and left that the institutions of civil society are doing badly: for example, the conservative (or neo-conservative) columnist for the *Daily Mail*, Melanie Phillips, writes that:

> British political and intellectual life is mired in a culture of despair. So-called progressives merely seek to appease the forces eroding social, moral and cultural norms . . . creating countless victims; while many conservatives appear unable to grasp what has to be done to support and encourage the most decent instincts of the people.

On the left, David Marquand, the social democratic political scientist, writes that 'in Britain, the last 20 years have seen an aggressively interventionist state systematically enfeebling the institutions and practises that nurtured [the public domain] and . . . as a result, it is now in crisis'.

I believe that both of these dystopian views are overdone, and are wrong in agreeing that the government of the day is primarily to blame for the evils which they inflate. In doing so, they play into – in Phillips' case, her view is an important part of – the dominant tropes of the media, while ignoring the power of the media to create the sense of crisis which they describe. We cannot judge for ourselves what and how norms are eroded, or how much of our public domain is in crisis, unless we have more media which allow us to make up our minds rationally on the basis of evidence which

23

will be, like political and social life themselves, conflicting, contradictory and rich in layers of meaning which media can assist in
clarifying – but presently more often mystify. We should not allow
ourselves to be encouraged to become mere spectators of a politics
represented by the media as sordid, drained of content and increasingly unpopular. We should demand of our media – and have
a right to demand of the publicly funded media – that they seek to
counteract the anomie and indifference to politics which they
proclaim by seeking to tell the complex truth and by examining
their own role in creating the situations they affect to deplore.

The media must do so largely on their own. Democratic polities
have put media into a special box, with privileges unknown to
other 'estates of the realm', protected by an acceptance of their own
(and others', from at least John Milton on) estimation of themselves as defenders of liberty. Jean-Marie Colombani, the editor of
Le Monde, writes that it is

> impossible to regulate, control or discipline the press . . . without
> putting at risk the very principle of freedom of expression. History,
> unfortunately, provides constant proof of this: as soon as an
> authoritarian tendency arises, the freedom of the press is infringed.
> Each newspaper must thus defend, on its own, the ethics of its
> profession, guarantee and regulate it under the threat of losing what
> trust the readers have vested in it. And to protect it from the charge
> of being an opaque institution, this privilege demands the obligation
> of transparency.

Colombani, in the same passage, also claims that newspapers 'do
not address themselves to consumers, electors or pupils: they
address themselves to citizens. They inform them freely.' The
two points he makes unite in the privileges claimed by and
accorded to the media: the privileges are claimed, and the right

24

of regulation reserved for the media collectively or individually, because of the assumed responsibility they have taken on to 'address themselves to the citizen' – and that they must do so freely, according to their judgement of what constitutes the truth. But what happens if and when the media no longer address the citizens? Or address them with information they cannot use in pursuit of citizenship? Or tell them untruths and lies?

As Free as the Society

GLOBALIZATION is partly an effect of the media, but it hasn't globalized the media. Media bring the world to us more immediately than has ever been done before, but they do so through heavily national filters. We have American, British, French, Japanese, Russian and many other versions of the world: the globe is nationalized many times over.

National media cultures remain very different from each other. They are in many ways *more* different now, four centuries after the appearance of regular printed broadsheets, than they were when these were first circulated. That was when merchants, state officials, idealists and radicals in different countries would support or write rather similar kinds of news. The people who produced the news of these times and the people for whom they were produced belonged to the tiny educated classes – with similar (at least in Europe and later in North America) education and world views.

The modern media are called mass media because they have reached the masses – almost, in all the advanced countries and many of the developing ones, to the point of saturation. In most countries, rich and sophisticated people are often mass media poor: they don't watch much TV. Most of the poor, and certainly the lesser educated, on the other hand, are mass media rich: they usually watch a lot of television. Conversely – a problem at the heart of our modern societies – the people who watch a lot of TV tend to be information poor, and the people who don't are often information rich. That's because the main TV channels give less and less news and information, that is increasingly to be found on specialist channels, in small-run publications and on the Internet, where Google has made it rapidly available in large quantities. It's also because newspapers are becoming more and more a preserve of the elite: and even the elite aren't buying enough of them.

The 'mass-ness' of the media means that they both draw strongly on (and increasingly powerfully create) the national culture to which they broadcast and distribute. They are thus very American, or Italian, or Swedish. They are nearly always spoken or written in the language of the country; and they are patriotic – whether mildly, when the national team is being covered; or enthusiastically and emotionally, as in the US after 9/11; or respectfully, when the national symbols and centres of power are being shown in cele- bratory or obituary mode.

The less you understand the media of a given country, the more they seem similar. The foreign eye, unable to understand the language, picks up on the similarities – the same Hollywood films, soap operas and comedy shows dubbed over; the same products advertised, often in similar ways; the same smiling announcers and emphasis on youth and beauty; the same newspaper layout and pictures. The *more* one understands the media of that given country, the more foreign it feels. With understanding comes the recognition that a vast range of cultural reflexes, references and traditions are constantly in play. A glimpse into the strength and depth of the roots the media put down into the psyches and sentiments of the people shows that the journalists, producers and editors draw from these people, and from the social and political soil, the nature of its media culture – including its news and current affairs culture. It is in that sense that a culture gets the media it deserves, though it can always, with an effort, make sure it deserves better – and sometimes get better.

Yet if there are many ways of doing – or not doing – news, there is now only one approved mega-model, to which very large lip service is paid. That model is probably best called the American, since it was developed there, and that country's influence on the model is still by far the strongest. However, it also partakes of strong British influences and many in other countries call it the Anglo-Saxon model. In the hard version of the model, the journalist has a function which partakes of some of the qualities of a priesthood: charged with telling society truths, providing society with a forum for a debate and holding the powers in that society to constant account. For such high tasks, persons of high responsibility are needed. It is the largest reason why, in the US, the training of journalists is most advanced, why the best journalism – in a few of the big newspapers and magazines, and occasionally on TV and radio – is so enviably good; and why the sins of journalism, as those cases where reporters fake stories, are so highly publicized and harshly punished.

The style also assumes a readership and viewership who share a desire to be told or shown the details of a given narrative as quickly, unambiguously and clearly as possible; one which is heterogeneous culturally and ethnically, and thus has no common inhibition on exposure. Thus, for example, the US Catholic Church was given full-length and (for it, as it made clear) cruel exposure over allegations in 2001–2 – many of which were shown to have been true – of priestly pederasty, especially in the Church's Irish-American redoubt of Boston. It was given cruellest and fullest exposure by a Catholic writer, Gary Wills, in the *New York Review of Books* and elsewhere. Any attempt to appeal to the large American Catholic community, or the wider Christian Church membership, to stand together against the exposure in the

29

name of defending Christian priests, would have been dismissed with contempt. Complaints by the Catholic Church's US hierarchy of media persecution *were* so dismissed. In a strongly Catholic country such as Ireland, Italy or Poland, such exposure would have been, till recently, unthinkable; even now, it is much more muted and diffuse. Indeed, as we'll see, advanced democracies such as Italy and France remain more reticent about exposing the sins of any kind of establishment than are the Anglo-Saxons.

Yet when wearing their Sunday clothes, all national journalisms in free or partly free societies embrace this style. Like democratic institutions, it is the approved global standard, because none other has the moral authority to describe itself as such. There is no longer any general acceptance of the kind of journalism Lenin was interested in when he established *Pravda* ('The Truth') – that is, a journalism which would agitate, educate and organize on behalf of a political position, in his case the establishment of Communism. Few would propose that journalism must put state interests before truth. Journalism with a predetermined goal given by another authority – to establish Communism, to liberate the oppressed, to advance the cause of a nation, a people or a group – is regarded as propaganda, or advocacy, not 'proper' journalism. It is, of course, at least as common in the world as the various degrees of independent journalism: but it has no principle on which to rest. The principle, and the test, is independence: the procedure open-minded inquiry; the context a free society which can tolerate independent inquiry.

But beneath the approved standard, very many different degrees of independence exist. Societies other than the Anglo-Saxon ones have different media practises. It's important that we know and recognize that, because the reasons why other journalisms exist and flourish throw light on the Anglo-Saxon attitudes which, like

English itself, are assumed to be globalized. They are a kind of test of their robustness and of the strength of our belief in them.

To provide some wider context for the problem we think we have in Britain, I asked a lot of foreign journalists, and others abroad who think about journalism, what their national experience was and what the debates were in their states. I limited myself, in the main, to the three rich democracies of France, Italy and Sweden. The first, France, has like Britain had a tradition of media enterprise and freedom for four centuries. Italy has, like Britain, a very large state-funded broadcaster in RAI – but also has the famously anomalous situation of its largest media magnate by far being the prime minister, in the figure of Silvio Berlusconi. This is a situation which many, on the left and right, in Italy and more widely, have seen as both scandalous and alarming for the future. The third has the strongest traditions of social democratic consensus in the world – part of which is a continuing, if now contested, commitment to public service in all journalism, as well as broadcasting.

The best simple description of the comparative level of journalism I heard in my travels and conversations was that given by the Italian editor Giuliano Ferrara: 'the journalist is as free as the society is free: and that's about it'. I think that is right, except that you have to add that free media can play a huge part in setting up a virtuous circle in a society of freedom and openness. That is, if the political power is willing to allow them to do so, or is too weak to stop them, as in the Soviet Union/Russia at the end of the 1980s and the beginning of the 1990s. At some point, political power has to retreat and stay retreated to give the media real independent space; and that, in many states – including the rich democracies – is evidently hard. And not only because the state power doesn't want freely investigative, inquiring, analytical, challenging media; it is usually because most people in the society don't want them either.

An example. My *Financial Times* colleague Gillian Tett, who was a reporter, then bureau chief, for the *FT* in Tokyo in the late 1990s and early 2000s, found that as a foreign reporter she was kept outside the groups of specialist reporters or industry cartels – 'kisha clubs' – which in collusion with corporations and the administration shape the news into what is the preferred (by the latter) version of events. But she didn't know how much outside she was until she got a story 'wrong'. The story is better in her own words – those used when she gave a talk on the incident to a Unesco conference on the media in 2003.

A few months after my arrival [in Tokyo] I started writing about Yamaichi Securities, a major brokerage firm that was on the brink of collapse [and in fact later filed for bankruptcy]. One day, as part of that story, I was offered a chance to interview the head of Fuji Bank. He gave me a great interview, which was quite sensational at the time, when he declared that Fuji would not support Yamaichi, even though it had traditionally been an ally and this type of support was normally expected to occur in Japan. The reason was that Fuji wanted to protect its own shareholders – most notably the western investors who normally read the *FT*.

I duly wrote the story and the next day Fuji rang me to say that they were pleased to have had the chance to explain their position to international investors. In other words, they acknowledged that the report was correct. Then, a few hours later, another story appeared in the Japanese media declaring that Fuji denied the *FT* piece: far from abandoning its traditional allies, this story went, Fuji was supporting them. Worse, the bank was claiming that the *FT* misunderstood the entire message the bank wanted to project.

I was furious and demanded an explanation. Eventually, after endless meetings, one came: a hapless official explained to me that when the president had given me the interview, he had never realized that the Japanese media had read the *FT* so closely. 'What the

President said was quite right in the English language but it sounded all wrong in Japanese,' he said . . . I retorted that Fuji was trying to have it both ways – the bank had planned to tell the foreign media that it was determined to look after the interests of shareholders, but wanted to tell the Japanese journalists that it was protecting the keiretsu [corporate alliance of which it was part]. That struck me as very naïve – and I said so. 'But we have different media and different ideas of what sounds right,' the official replied. 'The problem now is that this is changing.'

Tett had encountered the Japanese companies, and media, at a swing point. They were caught in a dilemma (which continues) between their own cultural traditions on the one hand and a mixture of pressures on the other. These include a global capitalism which demands increasing transparency in the interests of share-holders, the decline in strength of the Japanese post-war corporate arrangements and the desire of some Japanese reporters and editors to report in the Anglo-Saxon manner. As Tett said:

Japan just does not know how to 'speak' the American style language of media . . . or, to put it another way, outside journalists do not know how to translate the Japanese media language into their own [largely] American style discourse. The Japanese media culture still partakes strongly of the idea of a homogenous cultural framework and shared identity, where all the really important issues are left unstated; coping with cultural diversity – and radical differences in identity – is not something that comes naturally to Japanese leaders.

Nor, one could add, to most Japanese citizens. Coping with the aftermath of devastating defeat, two nuclear strikes, post-war reconstruction, very rapid social and cultural change and a rapid access of wealth has also meant a very large change in the assumptions of the media – which are, by past Japanese standards, inquiring and disrespectful. But not by Anglo-Saxon standards.

Ian Hargreaves writes of the Japanese press clubs that they

> are designed to ensure that both sides – reporters and reported – play by a set of unofficial rules . . . in essence a form of self-regulation designed to avoid embarrassment and misunderstanding . . . to western critics the style is, like other Japanese institutional practises, conservative, secretive and non-confrontational to the point where it represents a barrier to social and political progress.

But the point is – it seems that way to western critics. It doesn't seem that way to most Japanese, the consumers of the media, as much as most of its producers and sources.

The media in their 'Sunday best' represent an ideal of rational inquiry and open publication. Journalists who play by these rules must assume that the people they quote say what they mean and will stand by their statements in all situations: as Tett's sources did not.

Though I would share Tett's indignation at being two-timed as she was by Fuji, I know well the world view she describes – and not from Japan. I grew up in the 1950s in a fishing village on the Scottish east coast: a weekly paper served the half dozen fishing communities and their rural hinterland. Called the *East Fife Observer*, it was deeply respectful of – put another way, wholly silent about – the inhibitions, feuds, arguments and peccadilloes which any inquiring and diligent reporter could have dug out in a day or two of talking. When, seeking to start my career as a journalist early, I took the editor/publisher schoolboy articles, he put aside those which could cause any offence, and published only those which could cause none. No one I know of in the area thought this was reprehensible or wrong: they thought the paper was a bit dull, but not that it was failing them. The paper was a free paper in a free society in which the society of the fishing villages and its inhibitions curbed local press inquiry and controversy. Controversy and inquiry there were – but it happened elsewhere, in the political debate (lively, at times); in the arguments between individuals and groups (often animated); in the oversight of neighbours and community leaders (active); and, at an extreme, the attention of the police and the courts (light). Japan – more homogenous in culture and ethnicity than any other advanced society – has retained some of the attitudes of 1950s East Fife and resents their being disturbed and challenged just as much.

On one side is the radical individualization of the American reporter, with the refusal on principle to be defined or compromised by anything other than a professional duty to objectivity. It's an ideal which must be seen to be unsullied by an affiliation to another organization (than the media employer) which might provoke a clash of interests, or worse, a covert surrender in writing or broadcasting or editing to the loyalties imposed by an institutional loyalty. On the other side is the corporate/national loyalty of the Japanese reporter, continually conscious of the inhibitions freely or otherwise entered into by membership of his professional circle, willing or able to publish only an agreed version of events and facts which is far from the sum of his knowledge.

It is a large part of the argument of this essay that the 'individualized' journalism – in which the story and the 'truth' it embodies is a product of the journalist's and his employer's judgement and conscience – is facing both journalism and society with many problems. But I'm not arguing that we should, or for that matter can, return to a journalism where the boundaries of what is said or

35

shown are laid down by the state, or are part imposed, part understood, as in Japan. Once you get to the stage of laws and regulations on what can be said, there is often – as Jean-Marie Colombani observed (see p. 24 of the Introduction) – no way back.

Nor, for those societies in which media freedom is well established – as in Britain – is there any demand for a way back. Politicians and officials, corporate managers and voluntary activists, form a complex support group-web for independent media. If they were all pursuing their pure corporate or individual interests, they might want the media under different kinds of institutional or state control. But they have largely internalized the fact that the media should be independent, and frame their strategies accordingly. Thus what pressure there is for general, government-imposed curbs is confined to such things as violence in early evening TV or pornography on the Internet.

British public figures have bought in ideologically and temperamentally to the liberal order of media; in world terms they are thus, with a few other societies, unusual. The liberal order is the only one they will support; it is, crucially, the only order possible for the BBC, if it is to continue to have its licence fee approved by parliament. The only nationally influential figures in the UK who seemed to genuinely wish to put the media under a fundamentally different order were on the far left, and were influential two decades ago. These were, most notably, Tony Benn, former Labour cabinet minister and Arthur Scargill, president of the National Union of Mineworkers and an important political figure before and during the 1984–5 miners' strike. In the 1970s and 1980s, both spoke often of the need for either a nationalized media or media under some form of popular control. At that time, many people listened to and some agreed with them. Now, people don't care much about their message; Tony Benn has recast himself as

36

loveable, and Arthur Scargill as a declared Leninist – radically different strategies for coping with age and powerlessness.

The direction which Tett describes as that now being taken by the Japanese media – a jerky move towards more independence – is likely to continue to be endorsed by more and more Japanese journalists, because it offers them greater status. It also holds out the promise of more transparency in an economy and society where key figures recognize the need for it, such as the current (2004) prime minister, Junichiro Koizumi. He sees the need for it – in some measure at least – because he wants to move society away from a corporatist polity to a more open one, in response to the economic depression which dogged Japan for over a decade. Journalism can help in that; or at least it's an inevitable accompaniment to reform, since the culture which produces agreed versions of events, and goes so far as to do one version for foreigners and another for Japanese, can't survive in a more open world.

Journalists interpret the events which they reveal; they cannot help but do so, if in no other way than by the simple act of selecting which events to reveal and how to order them. The best part of the Anglo-Saxon model of journalism is that it holds the promise that journalists should and can interpret the world for all the population, and that it provides platforms – press, radio, TV – for clashing opinions, especially those which dissent from the policies of power. Journalists give the first draft of history: historians may do a quite different draft, but most people don't read the histories – so for them it's the first and last.

French journalism has great traditions, as great as those of Britain (see pp. 144–6). But many French journalists have told me that it suffers from a crisis of complicity; and some of the examples they produced for that give some evidence of it. Journalism in France has to have a relationship with a state, senior politicians and

37

officials much stronger, and much more sure of their rights, privileges and their dignity, than in Britain – and, at least in relation to the media, the United States and Germany.

One example tells the story better than any other. Each year, on 14 July – Bastille Day – the President of the Republic (currently Jacques Chirac) is interviewed on television by two journalists. Everything about the occasion points to the dominance of the state. The president is interviewed on the state's most important anniversary; one of his other principal duties on that day is to review a march past of the French armed forces parading down the Champs Elysées. He is interviewed in a room of his official residence, the Elysée Palace. The interviewers are chosen by him. The contrast with the British prime minister, only rarely interviewed in Downing Street (in any case much less magnificient than the Elysée) and sometimes, recently, confronted with an audience of electors chosen for their scepticism, is stark. Further, the custom in an interview with the president – and, for the most part, with the French prime minister and other ministers – is for one question on one theme only. Thus the interviewer can ask a difficult or delicate question of the president, but there's no follow-up. The British prime minister is interviewed on the media's territory and on their terms: the French president on his territory and his terms (the president is, of course, head of state as well as – when a government of his own party is in power, as has been the case with Chirac since the elections of 2002 – de facto of the government).

The interview, in any form, is tremendously important to the politician, because it is the main opportunity other than a speech (which will rarely be broadcast or reported in full) to speak directly to an electorate. French politicians – and other public figures – who do an interview in a newspaper get the questions and the answers reproduced, sometimes in full and always with the main points given prominence. In the case of Le Monde – the practise is copied elsewhere – a copy of the interview is seen by the interviewee, who is allowed to make changes to it before publication. In France – and elsewhere – politicians have been allowed to keep control of the interview; in Britain, the journalists have control. In British newspapers and broadcasts, usually only that part of what may be a long interview, which is in accord with the impression the story wishes to create, is used.

This is a central example, for it shows that an important feature of journalism that is convenient to public figures can also be convenient to, and good for, the audience. The British approach to interviews is not, generally, to reproduce them in question-and-answer written form, but to comb the answers for the most salient comments and revelations and use them in the construction of a story. This has the merit of privileging the most interesting (in the view of the journalist) parts of the interview. It does not, however, allow the public figure to represent policies, programmes and actions as she or he wishes (and on which she or he will then tend to act) and it narrows, sometimes dramatically and dramatically unfairly, the scope of the interview. The public figure is deprived of the ability to expound – a loss which most British journalists would see as entirely bearable. But the public is also deprived of the opportunity to understand, and to make their own minds up about, the explanations advanced for policies which may be of importance.

Formal interviews with political leaders are, of course, only part of the political story anywhere. But in France, they are probably less of the story than in other important states. Françoise Fressoz, who is the chief political reporter for the daily *Les Echos*, told me that

the curse of French political journalism is the connivance between the political class and the political correspondents: they live, work, holiday, eat and sometimes sleep together. I had been an economics writer [for *Libération*] and I was used to dealing with announcements, facts, figures. When I was asked to do the political job, I was amazed at the extraordinary closeness of the two professions, politicians and journalists.

The main problem is the off-the-record habit [the French for off the record is '*le off*': in 2003, *Le Monde* journalist Daniel Cartan wrote a book called *Naturellement, c'est Off*, which blasted the tradition]. You go to a press conference and you get a lot of official stuff which means little. You meet a politician for lunch and at the end of it, when he's relaxed, he'll tell you a whole lot of stuff which you can't attribute – and which may or may not be true. Nicholas Sarkozy [the popular and prominent minister of the interior in the centre-right government of Jean Raffarin] gave an off-the-record interview to reporters from *Paris Match*. In it, he criticized the Japanese sport of sumo wrestling as a mindless activity – a sport which is a favourite of President Jacques Chirac. *Paris Match*, seeing a way to turn up the heat on the clear rivalry between Chirac and the young pretender Sarkozy, printed it, and he immediately denied he'd ever said it. And the magazine was held to be at fault: not him.

Thomas Ferenczi, the associate editor of *Le Monde*, said there was 'a real danger for democracy here; namely, that journalists and politicians, because they are so closely linked, have their own narrow idea of what the media should cover – namely the "political microcosm" in which "hyperambitious people with no conviction" compete with each other and ignore the interests of the people'.

Perhaps because they can be more insouciant about a much lower decibel press, French politicians do not hire journalists to be their media directors, or shields; British politicians increasingly do. Alastair Campbell, the prime minister's director of communications, was a tabloid journalist, as a political writer for the Mirror group of newspapers: Philip Bassett, a speechwriter and strategist in No 10, had been a journalist for the *FT*, *The Times* and the BBC; John Williams, who became head of Foreign Office communications in 1999, had been an *Evening Standard* and *Daily Mirror* writer; Martin Sixsmith, head of communications at the Department of Health (who parted with bitterness after an internal row in 2002), had been a BBC correspondent; Sian Jarvis, head of communications for the Department of Health since 2001, had been a TV reporter. Their French equivalents are normally civil servants or diplomats; occasionally, a minister will hire a public relations consultant as media director. The choice reflects a sharp difference: the British public relations people are concerned with the day's or the next day's headline or news bulletin, doing as much as possible to make it favourable to the government, or at least doing their best to mitigate the damage. Their French colleagues are there to get to know the journalists important to their employers; to take them on trips, invite them to events, talk them through projects in which the minister is interested. The French don't feel the need of daily protection; the British do.

Television in France has changed a great deal, in ways similar to most other TV services. That is, it became less – much less – official and respectful and much more demotic. Like many intellectuals, the late Pierre Bourdieu hated the French media – he also hated those intellectuals, such as Bernard Henri-Levy, who loved the media – and in 1996, he wrote a philippic *On Television and Journalism*, which sold some 300,000 copies and was the subject of fierce debates in the media for months. He described the process thus:

in the 1950s, television in France was openly cultural: it used its monopoly to influence virtually every product that laid claim to high cultural status (documentaries, adaptations of the classics, cultural debates and so forth) and to raise the taste of the general public. In the 1990s, because it must reach the largest audience possible, television is intent on exploiting and pandering to these same tastes. It does so by offering viewers what are essentially raw products, of which the paradigmatic programme is the talk show with its 'slices of life'. These lived experiences come across as unbuttoned exhibitions of often extreme behaviour aimed at satisfying a kind of voyeurism and exhibitionism.

The scorn of an intellectual who stood in the tradition of Sartre and Foucault highlights a deeper than customary trench between the highly educated French professional and intellectual class and the large majority of people. The national newspapers are a minority pursuit; the regional papers are relatively powerful but many people simply don't take a paper and depend on TV for their news. The nationals, led since the war by *Le Monde*, are less regarded by the presidency and by the government than television and the regional press (where some of the larger newspapers have higher circulations). Their circulation, as in most other countries, is gently drifting downwards: in 2003, the five main titles (*Le Monde, Le Figaro, Les Echos, La Libération* and *La Tribune*) lost around 5 per cent of their circulation; the one gainer, and that slightly, was the business paper *Les Echos*, which had recently changed its layout and presentation to be more punchy.

The elite opinion formers worry about this, the more since they see their own economic base slide away from them. Erik Izraelewicz, who runs the comment pages on *Les Echos*, says that 'it's dangerous, this divide between elite papers and mass TV, because it could lead to a kind of populism: and in France, that's easy.' Patrice de Beer, who's an editorial writer on *Le Monde*, says that:

lots of people here read no papers. They have TV. The TV also became focused on society and pop culture – as is the news. It mixes up pop culture and current affairs. It sets a particular agenda: look at the last election [in 2002], when the TV highlighted crime; immigration; the 'inner city'. It gives people the idea that society is dangerous, totally corrupt. It turns them away from public life. It helps the extremists.

(In that election, the far-right presidential candidate Jean-Marie Le Pen came second in the first round, beating the socialist and former prime minister, Lionel Jospin. The extreme left in its various forms received about 15 per cent of the vote in the first round.) Henri Pigeat, the head of the Centre for the Training of Journalists in Paris, says that 'in the last 12 years, we've lost 800,000 daily customers; that's the equivalent of the disappearance of a big regional newspaper. Our inability to invest, to finance a modernization, handicaps us. It's a worldwide phenomenon, but our neighbours are handling this retreat better than we are.'

This perception of the problem is not one which much animates the Chirac administration. It still does the centre left: Catherine Tasca, who was minister of culture and communication in the left coalition government from 2000 to 2002, says that there was a 'voice of France period' in radio and TV up to 1970 (Bourdieu's 'openly cultural' time). Then there was a period in which the left and the right tussled over privatizations, regulation, creation of new outlets such as Arte, the French-German cultural and current affairs channel. Now she asks, 'will the next period be one of abandonment of public service?' Echoing the print journalists, the former minister says that, in the state-owned stations,

there's a greater and greater lack of will among the professionals to develop programmes which are recognizably and specifically

43

dedicated to public service. They're too often chasing ratings, obsessed with the comparison of their ratings with those of the private channels, limiting themselves to reproducing the tried and tested models from abroad, or from the commercial channels in France.

A French diplomat with a good deal of experience of the British media, said he had been surprised

by the power of the tabloids here and how much respect they get. Trevor Kavanagh [political editor of the *Sun*] is an important man: he was the first to get an interview with Michael Howard [elected as leader of the Conservative Party in 2003]. The difference one feels is also the relative lack of respect: a journalist in France interviewing a minister is expected to keep within certain boundaries, observe certain rules, both in behaviour and in the use of the interview.

He added a revealing afterthought.

There is a gulf in France between senior politicians and journalists which is usually unspoken but which I think is quite important. Many senior politicians are Enarques [graduates of ENA, the Ecole Nationale d'Administration, or another of the intellectually elite colleges in Paris]; most journalists are not. They are, if you like, different kinds of people; in Britain, they are not. A graduate of Oxford or Edinburgh could become a journalist or a politician equally, not regard one as a higher calling than the other.

Perhaps. But a reminder that journalists in France do regard their profession as one of some dignity came in February 2004 with, not unnaturally in France, a remarkable piece of industrial action. Journalists at France 2, the main state-owned TV channel, threatened to strike against the channel's news director, Olivier

Mazerolle and the news anchorman David Pujadas, because the latter had made a mistake on the air. It was an extraordinary mirror image of the Kelly affair: in the latter, BBC journalists demonstrated in large numbers and paid for advertisements in the newspapers, to protest the forced resignation of Greg Dyke, BBC director general, who had defended the story by Andrew Gilligan, found to be comprehensively wrong by the Hutton Report. In the case of France 2, journalists voted to condemn Mazerolle and Pujadas for a much less serious error, which had none of the consequences of the Kelly affair.

On 3 February, Alain Juppe, who held the multiple functions of presidency of the main party of the right, the Union de la Majorité Populaire, mayor of Bordeaux, parliamentary deputy and former prime minister of France, was due to announce his response to a judgement of a few days before that he was guilty of serious fraudulent acts. These had been committed while he was an aide to Jacques Chirac, the French president, when the latter was mayor of Paris. Juppe had received a suspended sentence of 18-months and an order to stay out of political life for a decade – a judgement whose severity had not been expected. He had said, before the judgement, that he would retire from politics if it went against him. The tone of the news that day – I was in Paris at the time – was fairly certain: in an appearance he had booked on the 8.00 p.m. news that night on the main private channel, TF1, he would, everyone thought, retire from public life with what dignity he could muster.

France 2 and TF1 are head-to-head competitors, especially on the main evening news bulletin, which both put out at eight. Indeed, Mazerolle and Pujadas had been brought in from the private TV sector – Mazerolle from RTL, Pujadas from TF1 – to improve the state-owned chain's ratings. They did, sharply at first, when they arrived in 2001. But the old inequality returned:

what had been a private-over-public lead of 42 per cent of the audience against 23 per cent in September 2001 had come back only to 40.6 per cent against 24 per cent in February 2004. Nevertheless, the culture they tried to introduce into the channel was one which cut against what they perceived as the over-careful, slow-to-react, over-respectful tone of public service broadcasting.

The bulletin of 3 February was a huge problem for Mazerolle and Pujadas. The centre of the day's news fever was appearing on the rival news (politicians of the right deliberately favour the private service: it also has, of course, the larger audience). They decided to take a risk. Here's the way the two news programmes went out that night.

7.59.04, France 2: News begins. On the screen, a title: 'Alain Juppe: Standing Down'. Pujadas says: 'Alain Juppe has decided. After the judgement against him, he decides to stand back from political life to concentrate on the legal battle. This stand-down will be in stages . . . Emotion and disarray in the UMP . . . In the face of this political earthquake, three questions to Philippe Douste-Blazy, who will be one of the "replacements" for Alain Juppe at the head of the UMP.'

7.59.05, TF1: Patrick Poivre d'Arvor begins the TF1 news, in which M. Juppe is the guest. Before the interview, he introduces two separate reports.

8.00.50, France 2: Pujadas introduces his first report: 'Alain Juppe is about to stand down. So says the UMP deputy Patrick Ollier. It's also the feeling of all those we talked to today . . . the day's events . . .'

8.04, TF1: Poivre d'Arvor begins the live interview with Juppe.

8.06, France 2: Pujadas introduces a biography of Juppe: 'A career of 29 years in the service of Jacques Chirac is breaking off . . .'

8.09, TF1: Juppe says, 'So I have decided to appeal . . .'

8.12.35, TF1: Juppe continues: 'I would continue to exercise, I hope, my political duties at both national level and in Bordeaux, since after all the appeal suspends any judgement . . .'

8.16.40, France 2: Pujadas says, 'So much for the first part of our report on Alain Juppe's decision to resign – but stage by stage. He's saying that he wants to take advantage of the period of his appeal to organize a changeover . . . it's very much a stage-by-stage withdrawal because for the immediate future, Alain Juppe will keep all of his positions. So he's giving himself some months . . .'

8.22.44, TF1: End of Juppe interview.

8.33.20, France 2: Pujadas says, 'To return to the news event of the evening – the withdrawal from politics, but a gradual withdrawal, a partial withdrawal and above all, an inconclusive withdrawal, not at all definite, on the part of Alain Juppe.' A clip of Juppe's interview with TF1, without attribution. Pujadas says, 'So, from Alain Juppe, "You don't leave (*on ne met pas la clef sous la porte*) just like that." We await more details.'

The panic in the control room of France 2 among the news producers during the Juppe interview must have been poignant indeed. The account above shows that what they decided to do was to blur their own mistake: to rely on their formula of a 'stage by stage' (*'progressif'*) resignation, stretching that to 'partial' and 'inconclusive' (*'pas definitif'*) on Juppe's part. It was an obvious sham. Mazerolle protested the day after the disaster that it 'wasn't really' a mistake, but that he had simply 'moved the cursor on a bit too far, without getting it wrong'. But faced with his journalists' righteous fury and the government's disapproval, he went later that day: Pujadas was suspended for two weeks.

In a later interview, Françoise Hollande, the general secretary of the Socialist Party – hinting darkly at a 'media operation on the part of the Elysée [Chirac] in the Juppe affair' – took time to reaffirm her conception of public service broadcasting: 'The role of a public channel is not just to get a scoop, even if it's natural for the news programme to try to get the news before the others. It's also to treat news in the most complete and objective way.' Desperate to avoid appearing to agree too much with the government – whose culture minister, Jean Jacques Aillagon, had said France 2 had 'undoubtedly made a mistake' and that 'the viewers have the right to expect reliable, high-quality news' from a public channel – Hollande said that state TV had been starved of cash to do its job properly.

Though both the BBC, in the Kelly affair, and France 2 tried to blur over their mistakes in similar ways, there's a lot of difference between the BBC–Kelly affair and the France 2–Juppe one. The French channel committed the not unusual error of 'hardening' a story to make definite what everyone expected to happen before it happened – and then was embarrassed by a surprise. The BBC accused the government of deliberate falsification. But the most remarkable difference is in the reaction of the journalists. The BBC journalists – or many of them – thought that either there were no mistakes in Gilligan's report, or that they weren't important. The French journalists thought that the mistakes in the Juppe report were a fundamental breach of the public service ethic. In the British case, as we'll see, many BBC – and other – journalists thought that the boss, director general Greg Dyke, and the BBC had to be protected from government intrusion come what may, mistakes and all. In the French case, the journalists thought that the public service ethic should be protected against the boss.

This isn't to suggest that French TV does news and current affairs better than the BBC; I don't believe it does, at least not in the provision of good current affairs programmes. But it does show that a public service ethic and fidelity to the facts were invoked at

France 2 as the standard against which a broadcast should be judged; whereas in the BBC, the immediate worry was that any breach in the defences could not be tolerated. It showed, in that instance, that the more civic reaction was that of the French.

The French case seems to point to the dangers of a state whose strength allows it to be dismissive of journalists and journalism. In spite of the central place accorded to *Le Monde*, which occupies something of the position *The Times* used to in British society – except that it is always to the left – politicians can and do ignore the press and do not worry too much about TV. And when that happens, the media are deprived of the power they enjoy in Anglo-Saxon societies. The allegations of corruption which have clustered round President Chirac – the Juppe affair was only one such – and which dog French politics at every level are of course reported and discussed. But the media are rarely able to claim 'scalps', as the British media have, on rather smaller allegations or proofs of corruption. To matter, media have to be allowed, by the political society and by society as a whole, to matter.

There is no correlative of a Whig progression of history in the media – that is, that they are destined to get more and more enlightening, independent and responsible as the barriers to that goal drop away. As Catherine Tasca suggests, a lot of the evidence points the other way: it does everywhere. In fact, the present evidence is that retreat from high reporting standards – or from any reporting standards – is more obvious than the advance. The most prominent case of that happening in an advanced country is in Italy. It offers the clearest example among such countries of media which have been tamed by politics. But it isn't a simple story and there are no simple morals, or simple villains.

Since 1994, either the government or the opposition in Italy has been headed by a media magnate – Silvio Berlusconi, owner of

Mediaset, the country's largest media corporation. When he was briefly prime minister in 1994, and became so again in 2000, with a huge and apparently stable majority, he was owner of the three TV channels of his Mediaset corporation; and he became ruler of RAI, the state TV (also with three channels). 'When a new government comes in, it commands RAI: there is a total and instant change,' says Gad Lerner, a long-time current affairs presenter, now on La Sette (Channel 7) the one national – and very small – channel which escapes the duopoly of RAI and Mediaset. 'There is no exception to this rule: who wins, gets RAI.'

The exercise of power is clearer and more clearly pursued in Italy than in other democratic states – less constrained and more a subject of dispassionate, as well as passionate, reflection. Media are about power: the power to tell the story of and for the world, a power which must always put them in contest with politics. Democratic politics should always be on top: they guarantee our freedoms, including freedom for the media. But when politics wins the contest with no holds barred, it does something like what's happening in Italy.

Italy achieved stability after the war by developing a careful and civilized (compared to its immediate past) balance between the political forces, one in which the media played a central part. The anti-Communist and anti-fascist Christian Democrats dominated the post-war political landscape; and the one-channel television service of RAI was conservative, decorous and Catholic. It remained so until the 1960s, when a second channel was added; a third came in the 1980s. In the spirit of inclusion, these channels were 'given' to the socialists (RAI 2) and to the Communists (RAI 3). The first channel remained at once the more official and more popular; the second a little more offbeat, trendy; the third more cerebral, socially concerned, leftist. All were, to a greater or lesser degree, rather formal, or at least so it seems in retrospect.

The person who told me much about how RAI worked, and still works, was its president, Lucia Annunziata. She is one of the most extraordinary figures in Italy. A woman of the left – indeed, originally of the far left, having begun her journalism on the left-of-the-Communist Party daily *Il Manifesto*, still in vigorous life – she spent many years abroad as a foreign correspondent, finally for *Corriere della Sera*. In the early 1990s, she was made director of news at RAI 3 – the left channel – but resigned after two years because of a fight with the powerful unions, a fight which, she says, diluted her enthusiasm for the left. She then joined Associated Press to run its Ap. Biscom business, until in 2003, Berlusconi offered her the job of RAI chairman. His refusal to deal with his conflict of interests had led the two opposition nominees on the five-person governing board to resign; they were replaced by nominees from his own coalition parties – with the presidency and chairmanship of the board being offered to Annunziata.

Annunziata has travelled some way, ideologically as well as professionally. The young leftist who helped pursue a system in crisis until it collapsed has been replaced by a senior executive at once embattled and reflective. She remains on the centre left. Just before she was appointed, she published a little book entitled *NO: the Second Iraqi War and the Doubts of the West*. The book directly contradicted the line of the Berlusconi government, which was in strong moral – though not in the course of the war physical – support of the British-American invasion. At RAI, she tries to defend what she can of what she sees as RAI's public balance; at the same time, she has developed a view of the political/media environment which seeks to understand the Berlusconi phenomenon without endorsing it.

RAI was a subsystem of politics. Until Berlusconi came, it was a totally dominating subsystem of politics, a monopoly. Very protected. Yet within RAI – this huge cow – everyone was allowed some milk, with channels for the Christian Democrats, the Communists and for the socialists. This headquarters building represents a huge national political power. Even now [2004] RAI has about 50 per cent of the market – with an income of Eu5bn, half from state, half advertising. We're still too big – Berlusconi is right about that.

When Mediaset was created, the breaking of its monopoly did assist the modernization of our television. The problem was that when Berlusconi entered politics without giving up Mediaset, he created in this country a system of control that is much less democratic than the previous Christian Democratic era.

The collapse of the post-war political system in the early 1990s saw a very large surge in the power of the media. They were the driving force behind the Clean Hands (anti-corruption) movement. The magistrates developed an intimate relationship with the media and journalists; indictments were on the front page of all the newspapers and were top of the TV news bulletins. Most of the trials 'happened' first in the papers. The magistrates were interpreting a moral outrage on the part of the people, but they were a highly politicized group and had been for many years. Many of the older ones had been fascists. Many were Christian Democrats. The new generation of the 1960s, coming into the magistracy in the 1970s and 1980s, were leftist and there is no question that the new generation were much more to the left than to the right.

Politics, shattered, had to reassert themselves, and they did, as most of the left renounced any kind of revolutionary road and embraced democratic centre leftism, and the right was reformed round the creation of Silvio Berlusconi's Forza Italia. Antonio Polito, editor of the leftist daily *Il Riformista* – who was an editor and writer on the political desk of *La Repubblica* at the time – now interprets the period as one in which the magistrates and the media, even if genuinely concerned with the interests of justice and equity, overreached themselves. He thinks that 'the left believed it would come to power through the courts – assisted by the media.'

In 1993, Giulio Andreotti – who had been several times Italian prime minister – was informed he was under investigation for links with the Mafia. The next year, Silvio Berlusconi came to power with a party – Forza Italia – created a few months before, bolstered by alliances with the secessionist Northern League and the centralist Alleanza Nazionale, the party into which the former fascists had metamorphosed. The party was launched with a videocassette, recorded at Berlusconi's villa, and shown on his own channels as well as those of RAI, in which he said that 'it is essential that there emerges a "pole of liberty" in opposition to the left-wing cartel, a pole which is capable of attracting to it the best of an Italy which is honest, reasonable, modern.' The themes had been largely chosen by marketing experts: 'never in Italy,' writes Paul Ginsborg, the leading anglophone historian of contemporary Italy, 'had the creation of a political force been studied so minutely and scientifically, and never before had it assumed the form of a party so closely linked to a single business enterprise.'

Berlusconi saw the judges as an enemy he must tame, accusing them of 'communism' and of concentrating their fire on the right and on business. They took a spectacular revenge: on 22 November 1994, he was wakened to be handed the morning's *Corriere della Sera*, which carried the news that he was to be investigated. Later that day – as he was presiding over a meeting of the Group of Seven leading industrial states in Naples (the subject of the meeting was organized crime) – he was handed a notice informing him he was under investigation by Milanese magistrates on possible charges of corruption.

Politics had been reconstituted in a wholly modern way, which means it was reconstituted on the basis of the time's most potent force, the mass media. The journalist nearest to the heart of Italian media power is Giuliano Ferrara, a former Communist, minister (for relations with the parliament) in the first Berlusconi government of 1994, invited to be minister of culture in the second, but preferring instead to run, in *Il Foglio*, a daily paper of opinion, polemic and squib-like news (supported by Berlusconi through his wife); a unique concoction which closely mirrors his own acerbic, challenging style.

> The total destruction of the party system left an open space, filled initially by journalism, but sooner or later you had to have politics again. And only an entrepreneur who had created huge wealth and had TV behind him could go out and bring together a party, lose, then come back a second time. The system was destroyed when the judges said Giulio Andreotti was a Mafia boss; Bruno Craxi [former Socialist prime minister] was a thief; and then the Berlin Wall fell and the communists lost any reason for existing. So Berlusconi steps in to preserve liberty.

I said: isn't it wrong that the same man should be so powerful politically, strong financially and so dominant in both private and public media. Ferrara said: 'It's true, it's a terrible anomaly, but there was no other choice.' For Ferrara – a 'Marxist still in the structure of my thinking', as he says of himself – there is no firm ground for independence, only ground which shifts at different speeds. In Italy, he believes it shifts very rapidly indeed.

> I think complete independence doesn't exist. There can only be relative independence. In the Anglo-Saxon world [North America, UK, Australasia] – and the Nordic countries, and perhaps a bit in Germany and Spain but much less in France and Italy – there is journalism which is quite independent. The journalism of the Anglo-

Saxon countries is independent because of tradition – above all, of the market, being independent of government and the rights of ownership. The tradition of politics always makes for a certain kind of journalism. This can't be avoided. It depends on the business culture: in the Anglo-Saxon countries business doesn't have too many links to the political system. In Italy it's not like that. This is a mixed economy, and private business is very much linked to politics and to the state – look at Fiat, linked so closely to every government. It's not really a market economy in the Anglo-Saxon way.

Journalism and freedom of speech is guaranteed in Article 21 of the Italian constitution, but it is a John Stuart Mill kind of freedom, a freedom which exists as an ideal. It does not set the material preconditions for freedom. You cannot really have any kind of independence as a journalist in Italy – and so I decided on the one way of being as independent as possible – and that was to take part in politics: to declare my position, which is with Berlusconi as the best of all possible alternatives.

Ferrara is right about independence: no journalist can have it unless the politics of the society in which she or he works provides it. And it may be that, since there is in Italy only, a narrow base for the Anglo-Saxon kind of independence – which has more limits than he supposes, especially where newspapers and TV channels are owned by those with strong political agendas, such as Rupert Murdoch – then you must, if you can, choose the boss you think is best. In taking a position you are being clear with others and yourself about the limits.

Italy seems to have taken the lead in mixing TV with politics – to the point where opposition politicians have come to believe that television *is* politics. They are not alone: Antonio Polito, the *Riformista* editor, says that 'when I started this paper [in mid-2003] I said I wouldn't cover television, because this was a paper about politics and I thought that everybody else was obsessed with TV. In three months I had to turn around 180 degrees. Now I not only cover it, it can be the subject of the most important stories in the paper.'

Silvio Berlusconi had, even before he entered politics, been the single most decisive force in changing the way many Italians saw the world, in part because he changed their language. 'Language became,' says Paolo Gentiloni, a parliamentarian for the centrist Margherita Party and its public relations strategist, 'the language of commercials ["spots" in the Italian adoption] – direct and populist' – the language people might speak, and after a while, did speak.

Italian TV is probably the most politicized in a democratic state: television (and thus the ownership or control of television) has a huge influence on political choice. Italy had a higher illiteracy rate for some years after the war than most other European countries. Many people passed straight from a non-reading existence to the television age – with no newspapers in between. This explains, in part, why the country hasn't developed a tabloid culture (the one serious attempt, revealingly fronted by a TV star presenter, was a failure). When this was linked to the fact that the TV channels were constructed to endorse one or other major political current in the country, then it quickly cemented in place a situation unlike that in any other major western country: television became a direct political player. You chose your viewing by your political inclination or tradition.

This carried over from the RAI monopoly to the Berlusconi age. His three Mediaset outlets – especially the flagship Channel 5 – were and are seen as endorsing his politics, even when they, or presenters on them, don't explicitly do so. Mario Cuperlo, who runs communications for the Democrats of the Left, the largest party of the opposition, says that:

The main problem of Berlusconi and his TV is that he is in effect the chief editor. He provides a stream of messages which are directly related to politics, but are also about TV. For example – on the issue of the conflict of interests, that between his owning and controlling the TV stations and also being head of the government – he says: 'There is no conflict. My channels are diverse. I have journalists of the left working for Mediaset. I have a satire show which is very tough on me.' But that's not the point. Research showed that the people who watched Mediaset supported him by something like 2:1. The presence of anti-Berlusconi journalists didn't matter.

At the same time, the old system of class loyalty to the parties of the left and right has been heavily diluted. Gentiloni notes that where working-class voters were very largely leftist ten years ago, they are now spread equally between the left and right – as are the middle-class voters. Indeed, the section of the population which has increased their votes for the centre left parties are the middle classes – especially the 'reflective middle class', as Italian leftists like to call them: teachers, lawyers, media people. But though you can't tell an Italian's voting intentions by class, you can by TV choice: the left prefers RAI, the right Mediaset. And Mediaset is winning over RAI: in February 2004, a powerful symbol of that was when Mediaset's showing of 'Grande Fratello' ('Big Brother') beat RAI's transmission from the San Remo music festival – an enormous, florid event which had claimed top TV spots for decades. One reason adduced: 'Grande Fratello' was full of attractive young people. San Remo's stars are getting on, and its biggest foreign attraction was Dustin Hoffman, who sang his first stage song number, but is in his sixties.

This power of political mobilization has its limits. Berlusconi does not use his ownership and his political power in the way authoritarian states did and do. RAI 3 remains leftist: Mediaset's

Channel 5 can be challenging of the government. And much of the material on his TV channels (and on RAI) is the same as in other western states – drama, soaps, game shows, talk shows of various kinds, consumer advice shows and so on. Leftist politicians and commentators are interviewed; some are minor celebrities. News that is embarrassing to Berlusconi is aired on Mediaset, and on RAI.

But the intertwining of TV and politics, more advanced in Italy than anywhere else, means that no issue affecting television, or the coverage of politics (in its broadest sense) on television – or indeed anything on television – can be free of suspicion of conflict. RAI executives, who wouldn't be named, told me that Berlusconi's people put two kinds of pressure on the station: one, by making sure that its programmes lag behind those of Mediaset in the ratings; and second, by ensuring that the news headlines and treatment reflect the government's priorities. And the pressure can go much wider. For example, the independent channel La Sette (Channel 7) is owned by Telecom Italia. It has around 5–6 per cent of the ratings and everyone assumes it is not 'allowed' to grow further. 'If it does,' says Gad Lerner, one of its most prominent anchormen, 'Berlusconi can respond by cutting back on what the owners can invest. How? By keeping down telephone charges [and thus reducing the parent company's income].' One of the reasons why the parties of the left oppose political advertising on TV (it is presently banned), says Mario Cuperlo, is because advertising on Mediaset would enrich their political opponent.

Even if he wished to, Berlusconi could not escape the conflicts which his extraordinary position creates for him. However, he does not appear to wish to (some commentators, such as Lerner of La Sette, think he may, if forced to choose, renounce his business rather than his politics). He's the dominating figure, and the dominating political problem, in Italy; he's important beyond Italy because he may be some sort of pointer for the future. Vaclav Havel, the former Czech president, warned on World Press Freedom Day, 3 May 2002, that 'in a situation where there will be no direct political oppression and censorship, there might be more complex issues, especially at the economic level, that may affect freedom of speech [and] Italy might represent an early form of this problem.'

What form would that problem take? The idea that journalism would be better at governing than governments has a long, if largely subterranean, history. The clearest expression of it in English was an essay by W. J. Stead, editor of the *Pall Mall Gazette* – an essay written in 1886 in Holloway Prison, where he was then confined for publishing exposés of sex rackets. He thought that the development of the press had allowed reporters and editors to understand public opinion, and looked forward to the day when 'one of our great newspaper proprietors' would fund newspapers which, 'through an exhaustive interrogation of public opinion', would become 'an engine of social reform and a means of government'. Stead wrote:

> the journalist would speak with an authority far superior to that possessed by any other person; for he would have been the latest to interrogate the democracy. Parliament has attained its utmost development. There is need of a new representative method, not to supersede but to supplement that which exists – a system which will be more elastic, more simple, more direct and more closely in contact with the mind of the people . . . when the time does arrive, and the man and the money are both forthcoming, government by journalism will no longer be a somewhat hyperbolic phrase, but a solid fact.

Silvio Berlusconi is Stead's dream come true, in astonishingly close detail – adjusted for time and for technology. His television, advertising, publishing and public relations businesses exist on the basis of constant interrogation of the views and desires of the Italian population. He has striven for more than a decade to create a political system 'more elastic, more simple, more direct and more closely in contact with the mind of the people' than any government could possibly be. And his control of the explicit and subliminal messages which stream from television means he has more influence, real or potential, over people's choices than any leader in an advanced democracy is supposed to have. In a lively book on Berlusconi's power to transmit messages, Alessandro Amadori writes that 'there is being born a new type of authoritarianism, a "soft" authoritarianism, based not on coercion as much as on the manipulation of the consensus, on the semantic transformation of reality, on the control of opinions, on persuasion and social pressure through these new objects of collective desire which are the mass means of communication.'

This formidable power will be copied elsewhere; indeed, it already is in Russia, where a (for Russia) relatively soft authoritarianism is now replacing many of the fledgling institutions of civil society, and bringing the democratic institutions – parliament, executive, judiciary – under the increasingly stern control of the Kremlin presidency. The close friendship between Berlusconi and President Vladimir Putin – which saw the former, while holding the presidency of Europe, extend understanding for the latter's terrible policies on Chechnya, the opposite of the European line – is one between two men who have understood that as long as you have the mass media, the intellectuals can be left to polemicize and grumble among themselves. Italy is rich in small magazines – *MicroMega*, *Reset*, *ItalianiEuropei*, *Rinascita*, *Il Mulino* – which can be tremendously stimulating, but have circulations of between

5,000 and 15,000. It also has a number of big city newspapers –
Corriere della Sera of Milan, *La Repubblica* of Rome, *La Stampa*
of Turin – which are national in their reach and which are either
forcefully (*Repubblica*) or restrainedly (*Corriere*) critical of Berlusconi. But they reach the middle classes only, and they compete
with the conservative *Messaggero*, the right-liberal *Libero* and the
Berlusconi family-owned *Giornale* and *Foglio*, on the daily news-
stands.

Berlusconi has another advantage: he is not an intellectual, and
has few in his entourage, beyond the protean Ferrara. Italian
intellectuals tend to a cultural self-criticism which can be very
intense and scornful; approaching the cultures and political systems of older and more powerful states – such as the US, France
and the UK – with an explicit assumption of inferiority, scathing
about their own. After I had met him, Ferrara got me to do an
appearance on the TV show he does every night on La Sette with
Barbara Palombelli, a journalist of the centre left (and wife of the
Margherita leader Francesco Rutelli). It was the day after the
Hutton Report had been released in the UK, and we were talking
about the effect on British politics. Here was an example of the
BBC being judged to have made a major mistake, was my line. Yet
most of the Italian participants said something like: we would
never have such an inquiry here. Angelo Panebianco, a columnist
on *Corriere*, said: 'can you imagine any prime minister appointing
a judge to look into his behaviour? Opening up internal messages
and documents? And if he did, can you imagine any leader of the
opposition accepting the choice of the prime minister as a fit one to
be a judge of his behaviour?'

When the British writer Tobias Jones published his *Dark Heart
of Italy* in 2002 – a fairly sharp, if affectionate, piece of reportage
on the Italy in which he had lived for four years – he was received,
on its Italian translation, as a prophet by the 'reflective middle

classes'. So, too, was the reportage in the *Economist*, which more than any other foreign newspaper had criticized the Italian prime minister, especially with a cover which, just before the general elections of 2001, proclaimed that he was not a fit person to lead Italy.

The point, however – not lost on the sharper members of the opposition – is that such criticism, coming from foreigners and the intelligentsia, is hugely vulnerable to a populist reaction. The respect accorded to the educated in Italy – with a constant use of honorifics such as 'Doctor', 'Engineer' and 'Advocate' – has a flip side, as in all countries: a resentment of the pretensions, even at times the existence, of such a class, with its grip on the printed word and its long-winded explanations of the obvious. In Britain and in other countries with a popular press, the tabloids redress the balance; in Italy, only television does. Berlusconi's message – which ironically has been researched, developed, honed and sharpened with more statistical and professional care than most intellectuals can lavish on their books – speaks to these resentments and slights. Television becomes the engine of a virtual class levelling, in which the instinctual, the erotic, the comic and the play of fortune replace debate and analysis. Intellectuals, it says, are killjoys; and in any case, they have their channels – in RAI 3 and La Sette.

Television will always be tempted down the populist road, because it is more popular, and the ratings both prove that it is much more in touch with the people than the intellectuals with their little magazines, or even the reflective middle classes with their wordy broadsheets. Publicly funded TV does not escape the temptation. Italy and Britain have among the most powerful state television services in the democratic world. But the logic of the market has forced them both into going head-to-head with the commercial TV channels – and, in the BBC's case in the late 1990s/early 2000s, winning.

Television in rich states still must compete in prestige with the newspapers; in countries such as the US, the UK and Germany, the newspaper culture still wins out among the opinion formers and with the political classes, who watch little television and then only news programmes. In many developing countries – Russia is the most obvious case – television is much more powerful than printed media, which have either never acquired an independent or regime-sanctioned prestige or, as in Russia, are read by relatively few. And in those states where newspapers prevail, their circulations are in slow but continual decline. In their monitory book on the US media, the *Washington Post* editors Leonard Downie and Robert Kaiser think long-term decline is inevitable, because they won't be able to keep enough of their advertising revenue:

> if newspapers lose their economic viability, they won't be able to support the big staffs that are necessary to cover the news well . . . there's no denying that the traditional ink-on-paper newspaper is at risk. The biggest immediate danger is the decline in the quality of many newspapers. If they fail to provide information that is important to many of their communities and their readers, their claim on those readers' loyalty will weaken. And this is now a real danger.

Newspapers in all states will tend to go the way of Italy, concentrated on smaller sections of an upmarket audience.

What Berlusconi has done is to accentuate – he certainly did not create – television's talent to delight and dazzle and to downgrade – he has not destroyed – its ability to inform. He has helped change a country's language and culture through TV stations which were sexy, dramatic and funny. Since 'coming down into the field' (*scendere nel campo*), as he put it in 1993 – that is, entering political life – he has brought his own stations more squarely into a media environment which had already been defined as politicized before he appeared on the scene. But he does not do it with propaganda: he does it with entertainment, comedy and a culture which implicitly or explicitly reduces all criticism and all political discussion into a mush of voices which are manipulated to be part of the fun – provided by Berlusconi, in either his private or public guise.

Berlusconi has run with a certain grain. That grain is the retreat by television everywhere from analytical and explanatory current affairs, in favour of opinion TV which favours conflict or satire or revelatory reporting which accentuates scandal. That grain runs in all rich countries, after all, they *are* rich, reasonably contented and in search of entertainment. He, and Italy, are in a qualitatively different position from other states because of the extraordinary position he occupies as both the political and media boss of his country. Yet because of that position, he shows just how much of an understanding of the world's complexities can be thrown away by the provision of so much entertainment, which pumps out not a political message, but an anti-political message.

Quite simply, it invites the viewer to stop thinking, or let the screen think on his or her behalf. Laura Frontori has described the state most viewers are in when she wrote of people who abandoned themselves to television at the end of the day 'in a state of suggestibility linked to the fact that the person is only half there . . . for the man or woman, tired from the day's work, seated comfortably before the TV, the [TV] habit represents a ritual of passing from wake to sleep . . . an empty consciousness which leaves him or her open to the first representation she or he understands'. In that state, she writes, the messages pass into the mind subliminally.

Tobias Jones expressed something of the same thing in the chapter on TV in his recent book on Italy, when he wrote that Mediaset had achieved 'a degree of hypnosis', and that RAI has had to follow suit. 'Mediaset television,' he writes, '. . . has seduced a society to the extent that politics and ideas don't seem to exist . . . in many ways, the problem with Mediaset isn't that it's political in the purest sense: it's that it isn't political at all.'

The absence of politics – that is, of the complexity, the use, the necessity of politics for the maintenance of civic and democratic societies – is, however, ultimately political in its effect. Italy shows more clearly than anywhere else how the non-political has direct political effects – if the politician is prepared and able to shape it so. Berlusconi uses anti-politics for political ends; he has a unique chance to do so, because he straddles both politics and media. But elsewhere, too, including in Britain, the anti-politics of television are also political, even if not in the hands of such a master seducer.

Sweden was designed, in my mind, to present the greatest possible comparison with Italy. A Lutheran tradition; stable, usually social democratic governments; a continuous, earnest devotion to the responsibilities of public service; and a capitalist class which, though enviably successful in building world-class companies in electronics, shipping, telecommunications, vehicles and even defence, is concerned to be modest, charitable and visibly publicly spirited.

It is a culture which, compared to others, is clearly and self-consciously moderate. 'Politicians don't complain very much about TV,' says Malte Adreasson, head of planning at TV4, the main commercial channel. 'There wasn't a great fuss when we went tabloid,' says Gunnar Stromblad, managing director of *Svenska Dagbladet*, the second of the two upmarket Swedish papers. 'The debate about public service isn't very strong, because public service broadcasting is provided, and people think it works,' says Ove Joansson, the chairman of Swedish Radio – the state radio service.

The largest charge, now decades old (though it is made more from abroad or by foreigners than by Swedes) is that the generally leftist culture, permeated with social democratic assumptions and values, discriminates against the right and against business. The last, given the general health of Sweden's corporate sector, is harder to sustain than the first, but even the first doesn't have many backers from within Sweden. Commercial TV and radio were licensed by governments of the right, as in the UK. The two public TV channels, however, have always been generously funded with a licence fee considerably higher than that in the UK, and the state radio retains a national monopoly; commercial radio is only regional or local.

In fact, the sharpest criticism I met came from the left. Jan Ekecrantz, who is Professor of Communications at Stockholm University, said that 'the idea of a public good in broadcasting has now more or less disappeared. The new idea is that public service is serving individual members of the public with what they want. It's still an important ideological concept to oppose the commercialization of the system, but it doesn't have much force.'

Ekecrantz thought broadcasters should do what they did at the beginning of TV in the 1950s: that is, educate and enlighten. He said, disapprovingly, that:

> things started to change when Olaf Palme [Prime Minister from 1967 to 1976 and again from 1982 till his assassination in 1986] invented the second [state] channel, to give what he called 'quality competition'. But of course they began to compete on commercial grounds. So when one did a serious programme the other one did a popular one to steal viewers. That was the start of a time when the audience ratings became important and it opened up the space for commercial broadcasters. The 1960s and the 1970s were still very good times: there was still the old-fashioned ideal of public service, and people came into TV with that idea; there were lots of good documentary programmes and all kinds of advice programmes. But it hasn't been like that since.

He is right, of course. When I asked Malte Adreasson, the young planning director at TV4, what his channel's commitment amounted to, he said:

> well, we don't do many documentaries, I must say. We sometimes do difficult things on prime time, but we try to make them accessible. We did a three-part investigation into the sinking of the *Estonia* [a ferry which plied between Estonia and Sweden, and which went down with great loss of life in 1994]. We have just one weekly current affairs programme, for one hour, but it goes out at prime time, at nine o'clock.

Adreasson stressed that the channels do not schedule news against each other: the two state channels, Swedish TV 1 and 2, have news at 6.00, 7.30 and 9.00; TV4 goes out at 6.30 and 10.00. He said that though the commitment in the channel's charter to public service broadcasting is vague, he and the other senior editors would not put out a service in which some commitment to news and current affairs was not present. But, as he said, the channel was expanding its entertainment, not its current affairs side; it had added a new channel, TV4+, which serves young viewers, and was about to launch TV Cinema, a pay-movie channel to compete with the foreign film channels. Adreasson, who was a serious and careful man, was what Ekecrantz meant by the decline in values.

Ekecrantz was one of the purest examples I met anywhere of the expert who thought that public service broadcasting should more or less monopolize the airwaves, because it was good for people – and who sincerely regretted the time when choice was so limited that people who wanted to watch TV had to watch programmes that other people thought were good for them. He thought that most of TV was now meretricious; that politics had been debased by aggressive, flippant interviews; and that politicians were debasing themselves by aping celebrities – he instanced the then prime minister, Goran Persson, appearing on a cookery programme. He said that one of the most serious scandals was when a TV political reporter was found to have been discreetly taping long interviews with Prime Minister Persson for use on the latter's retirement, something which, he said, was incompatible with the reporter's independence. Coming from Italy, where the prime minister has it in his power to fix state TV to benefit his own channels, it seemed almost comically overdone.

In fact, Ekecrantz was only comic because nearly everyone has accepted, gladly or wryly, that TV is no longer like he wants it to be and cannot be again. Swedish media have two trends, rather more clearly visible than elsewhere because of the small size of the country and the compact nature of its main channels and newspapers. These show how even media which still retain an explicit commitment to the public service are being forced – or are forcing themselves – on to other lines than those laid down by their founders and by politicians, lines laid down by what the market interprets as popular demand.

The first trend is illuminated by an incident that everyone mentions when you ask about media controversy. Jan Josefsson is the hottest reporter in Sweden, the host on a weekly programme, put out by the second state channel, called 'Investigative Mission'. Kari Andren Papadopoulos, an academic at Stockholm University's School of Journalism, who has written a book about this incident, says of him that 'he's the most famous journalist in Sweden. He is known for being very aggressive and manipulative. People have a kind of love-hate relationship with him: they see him as an icon, or detest him.'

During the elections of 2002, Josefsson played a clever trick. Using hidden cameras, posing as an ordinary citizen, he talked to a number – 54 in all – of local politicians of all parties about their attitude to immigrants. Immigration into Sweden from eastern Europe, Asia and Africa was, by past standards, very high. In many cases, the politicians he confronted reacted to Josefsson's anxieties – he asked, for example, where he could get a flat away from immigrant districts – with agreement, or evasion. Only two – one Social Democrat and one Christian Democrat – had argued with him that his anxieties were ill-founded. The programme which Josefsson broadcast, four days before the election, in the 'Investigative Mission' series, pointed a finger of blame at the right of centre Moderate Party – suggesting, according to Papadopoulos, that 'the party had become racist overnight'. The results of the elections did not show that anxieties over immigration had resulted – as they had in other Scandinavian countries, such as Denmark and Norway – in an increased vote for parties of the populist right; indeed, it showed a sharp decrease in the vote for the Moderates, as well as a derisory vote for the far-right party.

Papadopoulos thinks that the trick was unjustified. 'Were the politicians giving their real opinion? Was it fair to draw the conclusions he did? Were the politicians not just trying to defuse the situation by changing the subject, or agreeing formally without meaning to endorse what he was saying? The conclusion was that they were racist, but how can you say that was justified?'

Josefsson was certainly putting politicians on the spot and in the limelight, freezing their less-than-principled responses in the harsh light of a report which implicitly condemned them for anything less than a refutation of the racism. Papadopoulos confronted that with the view that life and politics aren't to be judged that way, that coping with anxieties and racial fears isn't always done by answers from the liberal textbook; that evasion, compromise and even agreement might not necessarily mean that politicians were a race of proto-racists. Such an argument, she believes, points to the need to understand what political processes do: they defuse and cool through steps forward and back, and can be judged better by outcomes than by process.

Josefsson painted a picture of thinly disguised racism uncovered; yet the outcome of political choices was a confirmation of the rule of a social democratic party which was supportive of relatively high immigration, integration of immigrants into what had been a largely ethnically monolithic society and even positive discrimination in some areas for the new Swedes. Should not a responsible account have sought to reconcile these two realities – and make sense of them?

The issue, treated with a mixture of seriousness, discretion and defiance – in the latter camp, Josefsson was given a top media award by his peers for the programme – points up with unusual clarity the difficult ground between media morality and political accommodation. Media morality is relatively easy to come by: a principle on which most liberal-thinking people of left or right would agree is posed – 'racism is bad', in this case – and defections from the principle caught like flies in amber and displayed. Making adjustments in societies among those who see themselves as indigenous on the one hand and those from outside the country seeking in it citizenship, refuge, work or social care on the other is not easy. When done successfully, it is through a series of steps forward and back, accompanied by much accommodation of an un-elevated kind. It may be that Josefsson's exposure caught a sea of covered racism, but it didn't seem so in the choice made by the Swedish electors. The clash between 'pure' media and 'grubby' politics is one which all media cultures use to their advantage – the British as much as any. It's the kind of narrative that the media might be more doubtful about than we usually are. Not because principles can't be posed. But because practise can be more closely interrogated.

The second trend is in the press. Sweden has pioneered, in its own society and elsewhere in Europe, free newspapers, available every morning to commuters. The daily *Metro*, launched in 1995 and the first daily free sheet of its kind, has been followed by *Stockholm City*, both of which claim blanket coverage in the Greater Stockholm area. Like the *Metro* brand everywhere it has been launched, the Swedish *Metro* puts out 'straight' news, mostly taken from the wire services or other agencies – though, in the case of the Swedish *Metro*, columns and other features are beginning to appear.

The free sheets have had a rapid and dramatic effect on Sweden's main papers – both the upmarket *Dagens Nyheter* and *Svenska Dagbladet* and the tabloids *Aftonbladet* and *Expressen*. They haven't decreased their circulations much – at least not yet. But they have taken away a great deal of the classified advertising on which the main papers depended – greatly exceeding the amount they were already losing to the Internet. This has hit the weaker papers hardest – especially *Svenska Dagbladet*, with the smaller circulation of the two upmarket dailies. Gunnar Stromblad, the managing director of *Svenska Dagbladet*, told me that the paper was faced with its largest economic challenge – even though, in the year just passed, it had recorded a profit, had cut some 25 per cent of its operating costs, had ended subscriptions to almost everywhere outside the greater Stockholm area (because the large size and small population of Sweden meant carriage costs outweighed the sub-scription and advertising gains) and changed its size from broadsheet to tabloid, a move which had proved popular. Further, Stromblad had insisted on co-equality with the editor; he said that the era when powerful editors dictated the line and coverage of the paper and left managers further down the chain to sort out the consequences were over: 'the editor must be free to choose what he covers, but he must do so knowing the economic costs. I must plan the financial future of the paper, even while respecting editorial independence.'

But still, the pressure was getting worse, he said. The challenge was sharpened greatly when *Metro* launched a weekly property supplement, which it claimed to have delivered to every home in the greater Stockholm area; the move had all but wiped out the lucrative market. Stromblad said sombrely:

> There is a more worrying feature behind this. When I meet advertisers, they say, 'I like the free sheets because they don't have so much bad news!.' In other words, they are saying – the free sheets are giving us a nicer editorial environment for our products. Editorial departments are hard to build up and expensive to keep going. News is tough to get and to check. If advertisers cease to value news and analysis and argument set in a serious context then there is a very big problem. It is obviously bad for us but it is also bad for democracy. We play a certain role in the democratic structure of Sweden – an important one, I would say – and if we don't do it, who will? This trend is accelerating and people haven't recognized it yet. It will be the same in your country if it isn't already.

This view, with which nearly everyone in the media seems to agree, doesn't go wholly unchallenged. Susanna Popova, one of Sweden's more polemical writers who had been editor of the now-defunct magazine *Modern Times*, says of *Metro* that 'it has changed since it began. It's developing its journalism. The big papers don't want to recognize this. *Metro* people are *sales* people first. The problem with the big papers is that they are not sales people enough: they tell people what they should read.' (Popova, as she acknowledged, has an interest here: she writes for *Metro*.)

When I put Stromblad's point on democracy to her, Popova made an 'Oh, please!' kind of face.

Democracy doesn't need a special room to live in! Newspapers aren't the ultimate guardians of democracy. Look at the Internet – that's more or less free to anyone. Isn't that much more democratic? Look at the development of the internet: isn't it much more democratic? What people who argue this mean is that they are losing money and losing power. Media are about power, and that power is being challenged.

The internet has already produced a distinctive form of journalism: the weblog, or blog. These are do-it-yourself statements of opinion, or usually unchecked fact, on the internet, posted by anyone from real journalists, such as Andrew Sullivan, former editor of the *New Republic*, through would-be breaker of the mighty Matt Drudge's Drudge Report, which exposed the affair between President Bill Clinton and Monica Lewinsky, to – anyone. Stromblad's point that journalism in which you can have some faith comes expensive is the point here; weblogs usually can't be checked because no one is paying for the time it takes. The Norwegian journalist Olav Anders Ovrebo – to whose article on weblogs Popova referred me – rehearses the sins of bloggers according to journalists: 'They do not care for journalistic convention; they mix facts with private reflections. They pass on rumours without investigating sources and are generally unprofessional.'

But that isn't the end of it. Ovrebo also rehearses the sins of journalists according to the blogger. Journalists 'conceal their own subjective motives behind a façade of unimpeachable genre conventions . . . bloggers rejoice every time they detect a journalist's factual inaccuracies and other blunders.' Ovrebo thinks that bloggers, who latch on to established journalism with a mixture of greed to be fed and scepticism of the quality of the food, will be

73

a tremendously powerful medium for change because they will be the most knowledgeable, critical and active consumers. They will be destructive, in that readers will go to the internet and desert papers, but creative of new forms of communication. This at least is certain: the media must immediately rid themselves of the last vestiges of the arrogance they have built up over the decades due to their privileged position in society. Anyone who has stepped into a newspaper office has perceived that contempt for the readership lies just beneath the surface. However, with the readership becoming the former readership . . . journalistic arrogance will no longer be defensible. Just as the media have demanded transparency of politicians and business, media consumers will demand this of news organizations. To a much higher degree than in the past, media organizations will have to explain what they are doing and why they are doing it. The Internet, which some media workers still see as a threat, is perfect for this: to show sources, provide a background to what is done and to enter into real dialogue with the users.

Already, 'superblogs' are carving into the area once reserved for the press, and doing it at least as well. In Britain, the web-based opinion and discussion forum Open Democracy has since 2001 put out a high-grade mix of opinion, interviews, news and description. Since the same year, the net site Slugger O'Toole has done the same, focusing on Northern Ireland – getting several scoops in the process. Both actively seek continuing debate from their readers, who supply it in generous amounts. Both have some of the best opinion and argument around – which tends to be open and challenging because they don't have many of the hierarchical problems of established media.

Swedes worry about public issues as publicly as in any other culture I've come across, and their worries are both fruitful and apt. The cases of the investigative TV show and of the dailies' decline, both point up a particularly sharp and modern dilemma for the media – so modern that, as Stromblad said, most people even in the media haven't registered it yet. The decline of the newspaper is only in part the decline, or dispersal, of the advertising market. It's also the challenging of wisdom received from on high; the increased scepticism of journalistic conventions; the demand for more transparency. At a seminar on the media I attended in the spring of 2003, *Guardian* editor Alan Rusbridger drew a series of diagrams to represent one facet of the recent history of his own newspaper. The first showed a core of wise people despatching their wisdom to readers, who received it and occasionally wrote a letter to the editor. The last showed a jumbled, confused series of movements within a circle, with at the core a number of challenged people forced to reflect on their wisdom by a readership which had become argumentative. The *Guardian* has not lost its taste for opinionating, and that's probably a good thing; but for its editor, these no longer have the gravitas they once had, but exist in an agora of competing views which may be ranked in cogency but can no longer be dismissed.

It's a future which might include the end of many newspapers: even, the end of newspapers. It may also include an advance for democracy and for popular engagement.

They Will Gobble You Up

T HE KELLY affair was an evident struggle for power between media and government, perhaps the clearest we're likely to see. The power in contest was that over people's hearts and minds. And though the government was declared the winner by an eminent law lord, its victory did not seem, at least in the immediate aftermath of the affair, to have been accepted by either media nor much of the public.

Andrew Gilligan's report stated that a senior intelligence source had told him that the government had probably lied. In the words of Lord Hutton, when detailing the charge, it was that 'the government probably knew, before it decided to put it in its dossier of 24 September 2002, that the statement was wrong that the Iraqi military were able to deploy weapons of mass destruction within 45 minutes of a decision to do so and that 10 Downing Street ordered the document to be sexed up'.

That allegation was very serious. Andrew Gilligan, and thus the BBC, were saying that people acting with the direct authority of Prime Minister Tony Blair had knowingly falsified a document which was designed to make the public case for war. To do so would compromise not just the integrity of the secret services, which had assisted in the construction of the dossier through the person of John Scarlett, the chairman of the Joint Intelligence Committee (JIC) which sifts intelligence material for the cabinet and the prime minister. It would compromise the integrity of the government, and of the prime minister. The political consequence of the story would be that the prime minister would have no choice – were he to retain any credibility – but to resign. The government could fall. Not bad, for a two-way conversation between two BBC journalists at seven minutes past six of a morning.

The report was instantly and angrily denied by Alastair Campbell, director of communications for Tony Blair. The BBC refused to retreat or apologize: a position taken by Andrew Gilligan, by the head of BBC News, Richard Sambrook, by BBC director general Greg Dyke, endorsed by the BBC board, chaired by the former merchant banker and one-time Labour Party aide, Gavyn Davies.

Two parliamentary committees – the Foreign Affairs Committee and the Security and Intelligence Committee (which meets in private) investigated the issue, and found that Gilligan's story was not true. The source for the story was found to be Dr David Kelly, a government scientist and expert on biological and chemical weapons, with distinguished service in Iraq where he had been part of teams attempting to find weapons of mass destruction. His 'outing', prompted by the Ministry of Defence, was shortly followed by his suicide. Lord Hutton was then appointed to inquire into the circumstances of the death, in public hearings, which lasted through the autumn of 2003.

In his report published on 28 January 2004, Hutton absolved the government of all the charges of deliberate distortion which the BBC had made against it. Indeed, he went further, saying that in all but trivial ways, the government had acted properly and even conscientiously in revealing the name of Dr Kelly. Immediately after its publication, Gavyn Davies resigned. The board then accepted the resignation of Greg Dyke, which he had formally – as he thought – tendered to it.

Hutton's was not a popular conclusion: not with the bulk of the media; not with the departing Greg Dyke; not with many in the BBC, hundreds of whom demonstrated and thousands of whom paid for an advertisement in the *Daily Telegraph* to protest Dyke's forced resignation; not with the opposition parties and some in the Labour Party; not with the intelligentsia; and not, in polls, with a majority of the population. The people polled thought it wasn't fair that the BBC had got all of the blame and the government almost none. They thought Hutton had judged the matter as in a court of law – guilty, or not guilty – and they thought that the government was at least a bit guilty. These people wanted some criticism of the government they could get their teeth into, so that the drumbeat of criticism of the government could continue at a high level.

Hutton gave them only the possibility that John Scarlett, the head of the government's Joint Intelligence Committee, might have been subconsciously swayed by the government's determination to go to war; and the mild observation that Kelly should have been given a little more warning that his identity would be revealed. Even by the most inventive standards, it was not enough on which the media could run a campaign. Some media opinion accepted it, much did not – their reaction summed up by the word 'Whitewash', which covered the whole of the front page of the *Independent*.

There were causes – well grounded or not – for the media rage. The Gilligan broadcast of 29 May 2003 had accused the government of deliberate deception in a dossier setting out the reasons to go to war with Iraq, released in September 2002, but had offered no proof beyond the alleged evidence of Dr Kelly – which Gilligan had retracted in his evidence in the course of Hutton's inquiry. But many journalists thought the government *had* deliberately deceived the British people: they believed that Tony Blair had decided to follow the Americans into war in 2002 and looked for – or cooked up – evidence to support that decision. They had expected, or wanted, Hutton to give some basis for this belief.

The main player in the attack on the Gilligan report, and the BBC, was Alastair Campbell, the prime minister's director of communications – a bright and driven man of aggressive manner who willingly acted as a lightning rod for some of the criticism aimed at Blair. Campbell was a constant and noisy complainer about the media, and had become increasingly so of the BBC's coverage of the Iraq war, sending 12 separate complaints before that which he sent on Gilligan. Though Campbell had been mentioned by Kelly as the chief culprit in the 'sexing up' of the dossier, he was found to be blameless by Hutton – and was perceived, after the report's publication, to be gloating about it in a string of TV appearances. 'Getting' Campbell would have been very close to 'getting' Blair, which many journalists wished to do. Many more simply wished to get Campbell.

Hutton did not even make the point which seemed an obvious one. He did not criticize the very close relationships between the Blair aides – especially Campbell and Jonathan Powell, the prime minister's chief of staff – and Scarlett, beyond saying that Scarlett may have felt under psychological pressure to agree with their suggested amendments, which, as the e-mail traffic revealed to the inquiry showed, were many. A former chairman of the JIC, Sir Rodric Braithwaite, had gone public with his view that Scarlett should never have allowed himself to be so compromised, and it was widely expected that Hutton would agree. But he didn't. He named no guilty parties: except the media themselves.

It is a large part of the argument of this essay that few of the world's newsworthy events can be understood unless seen in the round. No action or reaction makes sense unless it is located in the network of events and environments which produce it, or sustain it, or destroy it. This is an obvious observation, but though it is central to the practise of journalism, it is surprisingly often ignored.

Context is often by far the most important thing about news. Any given event may be relatively easy to report in terms of bare facts – a speech made in which this or that was said, a bomb detonated in which so many people were killed, a meeting held from which such and such an outcome issued. What gives it meaning is context: indeed, the context chosen will usually determine how the bare facts are given – what excerpts from the speech are quoted, who were the victims and who were the suspects in the bomb incident, who said what to whom and why in the meeting.

Context *is* always a choice. The same incident can be transformed through rearranging the context: at an extreme, the perpetrator can become a victim, the peacemaker a warmonger, the official striving to tell the truth a bureaucrat disguising the facts. The most powerful context is often that provided by the news organization for which the journalist works; in this sense, context is the network of assumptions, political beliefs and moral positions which the organization holds. The reproduction of this context is done continuously and – among the most skilled journalists – almost unconsciously. Once the context into which the broadcaster or the publication wishes to fit the facts is ingested by the journalists working for the organization, then the broadcaster's or the paper's line can be reproduced endlessly, through all events. Everything is approached with an 'attitude': the attitude given by the news organization. Many such organizations are not monolithic: *The Times*, for example, has regular columnists who range from conservative to Marxist; the *Guardian* from softer to harder left.

There's a good contemporary example, in Fox News, News Corporation's cable news network established in the US in October 1996. It's a good place to look, because it started recently and so it's clearer from its broadcasts what its founding ideology is. On 27

January 2003, a Fox presenter named John Gibson called an anti-war protest at the World Economic Forum meeting in Davos, Switzerland 'a bunch of knuckleheads'. On 11 February, a Fox presenter named Steve Doocy did a piece about US representatives and senators who opposed some of the curbs on immigration then proposed by the administration. Showing a video clip of New York Senator Hillary Clinton, he said: 'Guess who's giving sympathy to illegal immigrants linked to terrorists? You're looking at her.' On 23 February, a presenter described France – which was then making clear its opposition to a US resolution at the UN – as a member of 'the axis of weasels'.

All of these comments, by news programme presenters on a station which – maybe with irony – proclaims its motto to be 'fair and balanced', came out of a strong culture. It was one established by the conservative owner of the station, Rupert Murdoch, and its more conservative president, Roger Ailes. The culture was founded on that most powerful of emotive bases, a sense of victimhood: Ailes told an interviewer, 'I think the mainstream media think liberalism is the centre of the road . . . up until the Fox News channel, if any conservative or even libertarian got his opinion on the air, it was viewed as right wing . . . the elimination of anybody's point of view is biased.'

This ideology means that anyone working for Fox knows what she or he must do to be a good employee. The comment on Hillary Clinton was not concerned with other contexts which might have been invoked – Clinton's strong pro-Iraq War stance, her relative conservatism within the Democratic Party, her Christian beliefs. All these, of course, would have weakened the sense that Fox was striving to give of Clinton: of a dangerous radical willing to put her liberal beliefs before her country's safety. The comment on Clinton was thus a brutally directed choice, basing it on her opposition to one measure proposed by the Bush administration on immigration, generalizing from that to create a charge which came close to one of treason.

Fox's attitude, or ideology, has the merit of being clear. All media organizations have an ideology, usually one less easily discernible than Fox's – sometimes, not even discernible to themselves. These are now more fluid than they were in the nineteenth and much of the twentieth centuries, when newspapers tended to take a position of loyalty to a party, and when broadcasting organizations were founded on the more or less open basis of being supportive of the state.

The BBC had moved, like other public broadcasters, away from loyalty to the state. It had embraced – in its Charter, in its guidance to editorial staff – an ideology of balance and objectivity. It was not there to support the state, it was there to report on it, to hold it to account. Periodically, it defied the government of the day, and made it look foolish. Kate Adie, a BBC foreign correspondent, reported on the US bombing of Tripoli in 1986, and was accused by Norman (now Lord) Tebbitt, chairman of the Conservative Party then in government, of being a stooge for the Libyans because she showed the dead and wounded killed in raids which largely missed military or strategic targets. Thirteen years later, the BBC foreign editor, John Simpson, stayed in Belgrade when it faced Nato bombings – and was criticized by Alastair Campbell, Tony Blair and a panoply of Labour cabinet ministers, including Robin Cook, then foreign secretary and Clare Short, then development secretary. (Short compared Simpson's reporting to staying behind to broadcast from Berlin during the Second World War – which some US correspondents, including the overtly anti-Nazi William Shirer, did).

Both, in books they wrote after the events, dismissed the government efforts with some contempt. Adie wrote: 'I nearly lost my job due to political pressure from politicians responsible for authorizing the use of British military facilities for the raid. I said at the time that I stood by every word of my broadcast reports. Every single allegation made against these reports proved groundless.' Simpson, confronted by attacks which included one from Ben Bradshaw, a junior foreign office minister and former BBC reporter, writes that he said, 'rather grandly but perfectly truthfully, that I had never heard of him, either as a BBC correspondent or as an MP. The quote is taken up.' On Blair's attack in the Commons – he quoted the prime minister as saying that Simpson worked 'under the instruction and guidance of Serbian authorities' – Simpson writes that had he 'repeated that outside of the privilege of the Commons, I would sue him and win'. He is much more generous to his employer than Adie, whose comment suggested that the BBC had almost caved in under the pressure to fire her; Simpson says that 'the BBC is more robust than I have ever seen it: I get calls of support from Sir Christopher Bland, the BBC chairman; Sir John Birt, the director general; Tony Hall, head of news and any number of others. In the past the BBC would have caved in at once. Nowadays it's developed some real lead in its pencil.'

The BBC had developed, in these and many other incidents of lower profile, a view of itself as not just independent of, but above, governments of the day; a view which included seeing politicians of all parties as self-serving. This did not begin when New Labour took office in 1997; it had been built up over nearly four decades of generally increasing independence and power – a trend it shared with other media. In the Kelly affair, this attitude contributed very largely to the denouement. It was and is as important to know about the motives and assumptions of the BBC in its many guises, about the state of relations between all journalists and the government as well as the state of journalism itself, as to know about the other contexts and issues surrounding the decision to go to war. Journalism did not just become the story after the government challenged Gilligan's story. It was part of the story. It is always part of the story.

By 2003, six years after it was first elected, New Labour was paying several of the prices for success. One of these was a tenacious and growing consensus in the media that the government was a phoney; from there, it was only a step to believing, or at least proclaiming, that it lied. Or if not lied – there were few to display – then it spun. Spin became a definition of New Labour in the eyes of the media, and its examples were increasingly the occasion for the staging of media aggression. One BBC journalist, Nicholas Jones, has written no less than three books about spin. In these, he accuses Alastair Campbell – his main target – of failing to live up to commitments he made to the Public Administration Committee of the House of Commons: by, for example, lobbying against Ken Livingstone, the leftist Labour MP who was to become mayor of London (as an independent); by ridiculing the Conservatives' spending commitments ('an insult to Mickey Mouse') and by taking a leading role in securing the defection of the Conservative MP Shaun Woodward to the Labour Party. In the sheer volume of his writings on the subject, Jones gave the impression of a government as one which could largely be defined by spin.

The basis for the charges of spinning lay in the re-making of the Labour Party in the 1980s and early 1990s – the period in which Tony Blair rose to the leadership. It had passed through a long period of unelectability, though by 1992 under the leadership of Neil Kinnock it had done much to re-present itself as a modern social democratic party, with policies such as high taxation, unilateral nuclear disarmament, large-scale nationalization and hostility to the European Union all toned down, or deleted. But for the radical modernizers, led by Tony Blair and Gordon Brown, neither Kinnock's leadership, nor the brief period John Smith ran the party before his premature death in May 1994, had done enough to put the party in shape to win. They had concluded that Labour must make the sharpest possible break with the image it retained: still dug into a labour movement committed to the kind of socialism its members wanted and much of the country didn't. Kinnock had tried to change it but – to his anguish – he couldn't convince the country that he had convinced himself. John Smith, never having been on the left of the party as had Kinnock, saw no need to move from his social democratic beliefs and (an irony on which he often reflected) remained further to the left in his policies than either Blair or Brown, who had, as members of the leftist Tribune Group, been in formal terms on the party's left wing.

Brown and Blair had moved to the centre. Peter Mandelson, who had become the party's director of communications in 1985 and who continued to set the style for Labour's presentation even after he became an MP (except for a two-year freeze-out by John Smith during his leadership), had underpinned them both with a presentation which focused on modernity and moderation. Philip Gould, an advertising and marketing executive, had become the party's chief pollster and, with Mandelson, the shaper of its image. Looking for inspiration, they found it in the New Democracy of Bill Clinton; seeking a model, they found it in Clinton's victory over George Bush senior in 1992.

Gould's testimony on this American influence – he was exposed to it most, and used it best – is revealing. He had gone to the US for five weeks to study the Clinton campaign. On 3 November, he stood before the Old State House in Little Rock, Arkansas, waiting for Clinton to make his acceptance speech, having won the presidency; a BBC reporter, Martha Kearney, asked Gould, 'When is this going to happen for Labour? When will a Labour leader be making an acceptance speech?' He records himself as saying: 'When Labour has got rid of high taxes and trade union

dominance. When we have changed as the Democrats have changed.' Some years afterwards, dispensing with modesty, Gould wrote:

> these Little Rock days . . . changed me and I like to think they
> changed – in part through me – the subsequent course of progressive
> politics. Nothing would ever be the same again. Progressive parties
> would stop being victims and start to be aggressive; they would
> regain contact with the values and hopes of middle-class and
> working-class people; they would start developing campaigning
> techniques that meant that the left started to win elections far more
> often than they would lose.

For Gould, the pollster Stanley Greenberg – with George Stepha-
nopoulos and James Carville, the principal creators of Clinton's
1992 campaign – was nothing short of a political visionary, a man
who recalibrated the US centre left away from labour and minor-
ities and round the 'forgotten' middle class, with the themes of
'opportunity and ambition with the values of responsibility'. A
year and a half later, when Tony Blair had become leader of the
Labour Party, he made a point in an interview with Brian Walden,
which, Gould wrote, he had 'been waiting 20 years for a Labour
leader to make'. Asked whether he thought it wrong that women
would choose to have children before forming a stable relationship,
Blair said: 'Yes. I disagree with what they have done . . . we
[Labour] know the importance of strong family community and
family values.' These changes were fundamental, and of very large
importance – even more in a UK than in a US context, since the
Labour Party, unlike the Democrats, was an avowedly socialist
party. When the Labour Party, under the influence of thinkers such
as the sociologist Anthony Giddens, began to move beyond the old
categories of left and right, it moved into a new territory in which
policies and attitudes had come to be seen as right (some of them,

as on social responsibility and crime, were those of an older Labour Party, which had not been socially liberal). In one of his more influential works published during Blair's leadership of the party in opposition, Giddens wrote that 'freed from an intrinsic connection to either left or right, radicalism reverts to its original meaning as daring: it means being prepared to contemplate bold solutions to social and political problems.' Blair, in his leadership, rarely used the words 'left' and 'socialist', but he continually relied on the word 'radical'.

Labour's fundamental change from an avowedly socialist to an actually centrist party – so far proven to be lasting – was pushed through and directed by a ferociously disciplined and energetic leadership. It was also accompanied by the kind of media strategy Gould and others had seen in the US and which they adapted for the British media. They completed a transition which had been happening in the UK for some time, and which had already happened in the US: that is, from seeing politics as a largely autonomous activity which from time to time delivered messages which the media could use – everything from high public rhetoric to low unattributable gossip about rivals – to integrating the media into policy and campaigning. How politics was presented was not, as many have charged of New Labour, as important as what politics did or said: the presentation was not the policy. But it influenced the policy. It was accepted that people had to be convinced if policies were to be successfully implemented and that meant using the media to inform them.

If you were – as in the early days of New Labour – turning the party away from socialism, you had to do it in public: doing it in public was the point of doing it. New Labour did not have a struggle between maximalists and minimalists in smoky halls, nor conduct an inner-party argument about the place of civil society in the building of socialism. It put the whole thing in the newspapers

and on TV. The public acceptance of the process – of all processes –
was an integral part of the exercise. That such an approach was
open to a certain kind of corruption – that of posturing for effect –
was inevitable.

The message needed media, but the media were largely in enemy
hands. Most newspapers were on the right, and had conducted
furiously powerful campaigns against Neil Kinnock. But that was
becoming less important: the media were not so much left or right
as ravenous – ravenous for conflict, scandal, splits, rows and
failure. Politics had become a spectator sport. As Gould would
put it when writing a panegyric of Alastair Campbell, Blair's
director of communications for a decade, the modern world was
one where 'political parties and other high profile organizations are
under 24-hour media attack . . . he [Campbell] knows that unless
you constantly feed the media stories, they will gobble you up'. The
image the New Labourites used among themselves – of a ravenous
media which would eat *you* if you did not feed their ever-open
maws – is a common metaphor. It is one most memorably used by
the American writer Adam Gopnik in an essay on how media-
politicians' relationship had metamorphosed in the past four
decades – 'the change from dining with politicians to dining on
them' (he also coined the other, even better, phrase to describe
much of media activity: 'spleen without purpose').

New Labour came to power on a wave of media acclamation, all
the while being more proactive in seeking media support and
decrying media opposition – often forcefully, to the sinning journalist in person. The most visible and aggressive of the New Labour
media handlers was Alastair Campbell himself. Campbell was
promoted to the status, in the end, of a demonic, all-controlling
figure – a promotion which, in the nature of modern media, made
him a large celebrity and was hugely to his later financial benefit.
When he retired from his post late in 2003, before the Hutton

Report was published, he could cash in on the fame he had acquired: he got a column from *The Times* (on sport), a TV series from Channel Five and a round of packed appearances in halls up and down the UK.

Campbell was, to be sure, a novelty as a press man. A former tabloid journalist, he was a strong personality, ferociously pro-Labour, self-confident and profane. He would dismiss stories as 'bollocks'; he had scuffled with Michael White, the political editor of the *Guardian*. He was, above all others, the man who had to front the proactive media policy Gould had seen in embryo in Little Rock; he had to make of the opposition themes of radicalism with moderation, patriotism with pro-Europeanism, fiscal prudence with a determination that 'things can only get better' into a coherent government message – more, into a government strategy.

Journalists, and many politicians, saw him as ruthless, manipulative and menacing. Indeed, the harshest – and sexually charged – attack came from the novelist Ken Follett, husband of the Labour MP Barbara Follett, who wrote (with Campbell the main target in his sights) that 'people who do the briefing, who whisper words of poison into the ears of journalists, are of no consequence. They are the rent boys of politics, and we shudder with disgust when they brush past us in the corridor.' The chief 'rent boy' was the subject of a biography by the *Spectator* political editor Peter Oborne, which catalogued many instances of double dealing and which saw in New Labour the emergence of a new 'media class', taking power for itself at the expense of elected politicians in parliament. Oborne, who put into general circulation the cynical insiders' view that Campbell was 'deputy prime minister', writes, for example, of how in opposition Campbell tried to have Andrew Marr, then editor of the *Independent*, fired from his post because he had opposed New Labour's policy on Europe: the most serious charge, which Campbell says is not true, though he says he did complain to the paper's managing director at the time, David Montgomery, about its hostile tone on Europe. Oborne also claimed that in government, New Labour favoured *The Times* with a series of links and exclusives; that the *Guardian*'s editor, Alan Rusbridger, would be offered stories if they would be used on the front page – or if not, these would be given to the *Independent*; and that broadcasters were bullied to change the running order and slant of their news bulletins – successfully, according to Oborne.

Nicholas Jones amplified this in his books with an even longer list of offences – including a lively description of a row between him and Campbell, when the latter objected to Jones' report, during the 1997 general election, on a threatened fire service strike in Essex. New Labour disliked the report, he says, because it would remind people of the threat of union power and the unions' links with Labour:

> Campbell was incandescent . . . 'So that's the story, then, a trade union dispute . . . that was a nice easy question you asked [Michael] Heseltine [then deputy prime minister], wasn't it? It was just a free hit . . . I just love the way you guys in the BBC decide what the issue is. John Major only has to fart to get on the news. If Blair does something positive you don't report it . . . what right has the BBC to set the agenda? The 'Today' programme is just a radio version of the *Daily Mail* . . .'

Bernard Ingham (Press Secretary to Margaret Thatcher), anxious to draw a line between his own forthright if caustic dealings with the media and Campbell's deviousness, wrote that Campbell, with Peter Mandelson, initiated a 'terrorist regime' over the media – commenting on their stories while being written, spoiling scoops of which they got wind by giving details to other newspapers. Campbell was, wrote Ingham, a 'Svengali' to Tony Blair, coaching him to become a 'consummate actor' in his hands.

He was also a novelty, because he not only defended and promoted the government and above all the prime minister, he engaged in the debate about the media. Most noted – indeed, the only noted – predecessor, Ingham, had been gruff, brusque, but in the end accepted by the media as 'one of us' since he accepted things as they were and believed – or said he believed – that there was a basic decency and integrity to the British media. Campbell thought they were awful, and said so. In an essay he wrote in 1999 on 'Broadcasting Politics' for Labour's discussion forum, the Fabian Society, Campbell rolled all the media up together by criticizing the broadcasters, and especially the BBC, for having been infected with a 'deeper cynicism' which was the hallmark of the contemporary press. The journey the BBC was taking in the wake of the press, Campbell wrote, was 'a one-way road to cynicism. When it dominates most judgements, the media's dominant role becomes the erosion of confidence in politics.'

In a talk in his house one morning soon after he resigned from No 10, I put it to him that the animosity he stirred, and the promotion of 'spin' as a concept covering almost everything the government promoted, were a response to New Labour's 'armour-plated' approach to media relations. This was his case.

There's something to that argument, but I didn't see it that way. It didn't look that way from where I sat. You have to see it as politicians experience it to get the picture.

The scene is one of increasing and ferocious competition. Media are insatiable when there's a frenzy on. When the Hutton Report was out, I had hundreds, literally hundreds, of requests, for interviews, articles, appearances. My kids had to go to school through packs of reporters and cameras. For the prime minister and for ministers, at least at times, that's a daily reality.

We came to power as a number of trends were becoming more obvious. One was an almost total fusion between reporting and comment – not just in the tabloids, not just in the broadsheets, but even among some of the broadcasters.

With 24-hour news, you must talk. You must fill the airwaves. Usually, talk radio is talking about one thing: what's in the papers. So that the media are constantly feeding off each other, and a report in a newspaper, which may be true or false, is rolled around for hours until something else comes up.

I have to say that we didn't comment on this much in opposition. It's in government when it hits you the hardest. We did change things; I hope we did. We had seen the Major government go to pieces under media attack, and seen that it was just incoherent, with no planning, projecting no sense of strategy. And we inherited a government communications machine which we were told – by journalists – was ramshackle, pulling in all sorts of different directions. That had to be changed; and yes, it did take a certain amount of pulling of strings from the centre, of use of power. The end was to project a strategy: very very hard, when the media are so atomized, so consuming of everything. Only partly successful, because of that; but if we didn't do it we too would have been incoherent.

I felt we had a legitimate part to play in debating what the media were doing and how they were doing it. But I couldn't seem to get that across. Yet I don't know how we could have done it differently, in a way in which I wouldn't become the story. Journalism became obsessed with spin, with manipulation, with me. When [the BBC reporter] Michael Cockerell did a documentary on BBC 2 on the Downing Street media operation, on spin doctors, he told me afterwards that he got more coverage for the film than all the other things he had done put together.

I guess I misread it. I thought that the spin thing was not so much about me as about the prime minister, to give the impression that I was manipulating him into doing things he wouldn't be doing otherwise. All that was nonsense. I was with him a lot: I talked to him a lot, but presentation did not lead him to doing anything he wouldn't have done anyway. I knew and know that to be the story, but it hasn't been the one told.

One reason it hasn't been told is that Labour, at least in government, had put itself in a bind. It needed the media as no party or government had before, and it hated them. This was, to put it mildly, a source of tension. Alastair Campbell lived in the epicentre of that: his abrasive, contemptuous style, though wholly his own, was also stimulated by this irresolvable tug between these opposing elements. It could work well enough in the three years New Labour was in opposition, before its 1997 election victory; in power, it was a balancing act on an increasingly slack tightrope.

As time went on – and especially in New Labour's second term, from 2001 – the contempt and frustration began to weigh more strongly than anything else. The efforts to woo the media, which had seen Blair travel to Australia to address Murdoch editors, and saw him continue to try to woo Paul Dacre, editor-in-chief of Associated Newspapers (*Daily Mail*, *Mail on Sunday* and *Evening Standard*), came to an end. Tim Allan, who had been a deputy to Campbell in the early Blair years, told me that 'the government spent years trying to be chummy with the *Daily Mail*. It only stopped [after the last election]. Blair sees himself as the great persuader, able to convince everyone. But they didn't want to like him. The government wasted far too much time trying to turn the *Mail* around.' Such tactics, in fact, could be counterproductive: once known, as they quickly were, they gave the media more cause to profess contempt for the politicians as unprincipled crawlers to their power. They also seemed to have little effect on the *Daily Mail* – except to increase its professed preference for Gordon Brown over Blair.

The belief that the media are at least as much a self-interested group pursuing their own – either corporate (broadcasting channel or newspaper) or individual (journalist) – agendas is not confined to the Blair government. Historically, the US administrations have set the standard for access of reporters to power, in a variety of ways. 'Access' reporting – where a senior politician, up to and including presidents, allowed journalists hours of time in interviews, and in observing some of the to-and-froing of government life – was developed in the US and followed up in Britain (it hasn't caught on much elsewhere, because other governments don't allow it, or only on restricted terms and only to journalists who are 'one of us'. In most states, including democratic ones, governments would find it inconceivable to offer more than an invitation to press conferences to journalists working for media organizations opposed to the government line). Compared with previous presidencies, both Democrat and Republican, the Bush administration has been more reserved. It has been more willing to stonewall, leaving questions unanswered; willing to reward 'good' reporting and punish 'bad'; and above all, much more insouciant, at least in the first years of the Bush administration, about the downside of such an attitude.

In a sustained piece of reporting on the attitude of the Bush White House to the media, Ken Auletta concluded that 'for perhaps the first time, the White House has come to see reporters as special pleaders – pleaders for more access and better headlines – as if the press were simply another interest group.' Like the Blair people – Mandelson, Gould and Campbell – who worked on, and with, the media, the Bush people didn't think they should take too much care to disguise their dislike of media practises. In the Blair government case, this didn't generally mean that access was denied: indeed, playing to Blair's belief that he was an able persuader and could command a journalistic gathering, reporters, including hostile ones, were given a lot of briefing time. Campbell also initiated monthly, on-the-record, televised press conferences with Blair which were intended to underscore the latter's ability to deal with anything the reporters threw at him – and which became, for the most part, non-events because he *did* command them. Bush, by contrast, was uneasy, stilted and evasive in formal press conferences and kept those to a minimum.

The Bush White House understanding of the media was and is hateful to the latter in two ways. First, it thought they were self-interested (in common with the Blair government); and second, it thought they were less important than they had been (which was largely not what Blair and his people thought). The Bushies' contempt for the media came in part from their view that the Clinton administration would court broadcast and newspaper reporters – though, in fact, Clinton and many of his people grew deeply disillusioned with the media, rather as Blair and New Labour had. The Bush aide Mark McKinnon said of reporters to Auletta that:

> there's a natural tendency in political communications to want to be liked by the press. By doing that, somehow you improve the nature of your coverage . . . I think this administration rejects that notion. I don't think they think it works . . . [reporters] are highly skilled at what they do. There's enormous pressure on them to get unique information. So an extraordinary effort is made to establish and cultivate sources. For people like me who get involved, there is an instinct to say: 'Oh, they think I'm interesting', when all they want is a source. So it's easy to be manipulated by the press. This White House has done a good job of understanding how it all works.

'Understanding how it all works' has meant, for both administrations, being much more critical of the media than previous US or

96

UK governments have allowed themselves to be. Though right-wing presidencies and prime ministerships in the past – especially those of Ronald Reagan and Margaret Thatcher – have been at times harshly critical of left-wing media attitudes, the relationships they and their communications aides had with the media were largely confined to routine, enlivened with occasional spats. By contrast, the Bush and Blair teams, in quite different ways, have developed a dispassionately critical view of the media and their activities as a whole, which they sometimes do not trouble to disguise. In Bush's case, this is probably more complete; though he is often said to be amiable with individual journalists, he has shown little interest in engaging with them – especially not the critical ones. Blair, on the contrary, probably engages *more* with those who criticize him. At the memorial service for the late *Guardian* columnist Hugo Young, his editor Alan Rusbridger recalled that, mortally ill, Young had written some of his most passionate columns, harshly condemning Blair's action in going to war with the US on Iraq – and that Blair had handwritten letters of several pages arguing with him, seeking to convince him that the war was a moral cause.

The largest point of agreement is scepticism in both administrations on how far the media 'represent' the people. At his ranch in Crawford, Texas, the president gave a barbecue for the press corps. Bush had said he didn't watch TV or read the papers much. One reporter asked him: 'How do you know what the public thinks?' Bush replied: 'You're making a huge assumption – that you represent what the public thinks.' In an interview with Brit Hume of Fox News in September 2003, Bush had said: 'The best way to get news is from objective sources. And the most objective sources I have are people on my staff who tell me what's happening in the world.' Tony Blair would agree with that, without finding it surprising that he should think so.

One of the effects of the 24-hour feeding strategy on the media was to infantilize them: to make them simultaneously dependent and sulky, even hate-filled – especially those journalists who exist on a lower level of the feeding order. At the same time, the media themselves had changed. They had not lost leftist and rightist affiliations entirely, but these became blurred and shifting, as had politics itself. The consensus which had appeared during the John Major Conservative government from 1992 to 1997 – that government itself, with associated sleaze and corruption, was the target, not a government of the left or the right – was too rich a seam to be deserted for long. When, after the attacks in the US on 9/11, the close alliance with the US became increasingly controversial, two papers of the centre left – the *Independent* and the *Daily Mirror*, both lagging their rivals in their market segments – gave over many of their front pages to daily howls of rage at the government, as a commercial strategy (which failed, in the case of the *Mirror*). This blend – of a largely splenetic media pack ('spleen without purpose' – except the increase of its own power) working for organizations which saw the attack mode as the most advantageous – faced New Labour with a breakdown of its model. Whatever they were fed, the media spewed up conflict, splits, rows and chaos. They were no longer media down which messages travelled; there was, as far as the politicians were concerned, no medium for their messages – including the BBC, the public sector broadcaster. This was war: a war of position, with the prize, trust.

The view that journalism in this country could be one of the causes of social malaise because of its aggression towards those in power in civil society is new – almost, unvoiced. The media had been held, especially on the left, as being unfair to leftist parties, Labour governments, trades unions. Governments could take it, and should.

It has, however, been a theme in the US – where papers and

television are less aggressive – for over a decade. In 1993, the American critic Thomas E. Patterson wrote that he – and most others – believed that 'politics in America is practised by a governing class whose members, within the limits of human behaviour, mean more or less what they say and more or less keep the promises they make'. However, the media, Patterson wrote, saw politics as wholly what it only partly is – that is, as a series of strategies for getting and keeping power. Thus any declaration or policy is evaluated much more for its strategic, political – or personal – effect than for its social or economic one. On this view, 'spinning', or even lying about policies, is naturally what politicians do to keep or acquire power. 'Since everything is part of a larger strategy of power, no discrete project, law or statement can be accepted as having an integrity of its own.'

This approach was amplified by James Fallows, in a 1996 book called *Breaking the News*, subtitled *How the Media Undermine American Democracy*. Fallows meant just what the subtitle said. He accused the media of confusing aggression with investigation. He saw television as a medium incapable of proportion or memory. And he likened the contest between journalists on the one hand and public officials and politicians on the other to the nuclear arms race:

> in which reporters don't explicitly argue or analyse what they dislike in a political programme but instead sound sneering and super-cilious about the whole idea of politics. Public officials become more manipulative and cunning to try to get their message past a hostile press – and the press becomes even more determined to point out how insincere the politicians are. As in a real arms race neither side feels they can safely disarm.

In 1998, Deborah Tannen, who is an academic expert in linguistics, wrote *The Argument Culture*, in which she argued – in the

99

same vein as Gopnik's 'aimless spleen' – that while media had in the past been vituperatively nasty, this had been with a purpose – usually ideological. A writer standing for one principle abused someone standing for another, or for none. 'The spirit of attack today – aggression in a culture of critique – is disinterested, aimed at whoever is in the public eye. And a show of aggression is valued for its own sake . . . though it is unfortunate for the public figures themselves, the real losers are the people and the nation.' In that same year, the journalist Richard Reeves located the media's self-delusion as starting from Watergate:

> the signal event in the self-destructive journalistic hubris in the 1970s and beyond . . . reporters took on priestly duties of the political establishment, stepping up to the bully pulpit of moral leadership . . . carelessly and systematically, the high-riding Washington press corps and provincial imitators diminished politicians and governors, subjecting them to public scorn. Our message was simple: 'They're all bums! Don't believe them! Don't listen to them!'

In 2003, Kathleen Hall Jamieson and Paul Waldman, of the Annenberg School for Communication at the University of Pennsylvania, wrote *The Press Effect*, which closely analysed the coverage of the 2000 election campaign and claimed that reporters had narrowed their coverage to concentrate on personality and tactic and – re-making with more detail Thomas Patterson's point of a decade earlier – maintained that they showed:

> a relentless focus on tactics, particularly in campaigns . . . [and] by revealing the strategies behind politicians' rhetoric, journalists may be attempting to make political actors more forthright and citizens more critical. But without an accompanying analysis of issues, strategic coverage leaves voters unable to assess whether politicians'

claims should be believed . . . if we learned that a candidate appeared at a senior citizen centre in order to make us believe that he cared about the elderly, we have no evidence that he does or does not care about the elderly, but the implication that he is faking concern is implied [sic]. Indeed, in experiments testing the effect of actual news coverage [it was] found that strategic coverage elicited cynical interpretations.

British press and TV news are at least as cynical as their US equivalents. They trash politicians at least as much. More so, for the structure of the British press is much more competitive than that of the US – indeed, it is more competitive than anywhere else in the world. Britain's press really is 'pressed': a score of daily and Sunday newspapers are squeezed into one city, London, from which they are distributed every morning. In no other capital of a rich state is this the case: newspapers are either dispersed among regional centres, as in the US, Germany, Italy and Australia; or are fewer in number, as in Japan, France, Spain and Canada. Britain's circumstances have led to a hyper-competitive press in which upmarket, middle-market and tabloids compete for sales which remain among the highest in the world, at around 13 million on a weekday and 15 million on Sunday, or readerships of between 60 and 70 per cent of the population. Nearly all these papers depend on news-stand sales; thus their front pages are much more important as attention-getters than in countries where the main papers are one-city monopolies, or are confined mainly to the middle classes, as they are in France, Italy and Spain.

Front pages have thus always strained to present their most attractive wares. In recent years, many of the editors who have composed them have come to believe that this means becoming more and more anti-government, or indeed anti-politician. This has been most marked in two papers, both formerly pro-Labour:

the *Independent* and the *Daily Mirror*. The *Independent*, launched in 1986 as a well-resourced paper of record, is now trailing other upmarket dailies and has suffered rounds of editorial and other cuts. Its front pages are often scathing anti-government editorials; its editor Simon Kelner has responded to criticism by saying that only campaigning papers get noticed.

The *Mirror*, for decades the indispensable tabloid supporter of Labour, has taken the same route, even more raucously. For much of the pre-Iraq intervention period and for some of the war (until its patriotic readership deserted the paper in large numbers) it launched itself against the government, and especially against Blair. Its editor, Piers Morgan, a former show business writer, is locked in a titanic struggle with the Rupert Murdoch-owned *Sun*, which sells over 1 million copies more. Morgan, who had wooed Blair and his wife Cherie socially, was incensed to have been scooped by the rival on the date of the 2001 election day; and more seriously, on the fact that Cherie Blair was pregnant (she gave birth to a son, Leo, in May 2000). In both cases, Morgan believed Alastair Campbell had given the story to the *Sun*. The Blair circle believes it explains the violence of the paper's opposition to the Iraq invasion.

The result is a paradox: a government which has been more successful than most others in the advanced world, with one of the best economic growth rates, an internationally famed leader and a weak opposition, is attended by an extremely abrasive media. Foreigners who observe the British media and know the country remark on the matter constantly. They see a media which is polemically extreme, rhetorically bitter and savagely dismissive.

The result is a media landscape which, though filled with more newspapers per person available throughout the country than in any other large state, has become increasingly monochrome in the opinions expressed about the government. And about the opposition. Indeed, the media did more damage to the Conservative opposition, at least in the short term, than it did to the Labour government: for in the two-and-a-half-year leadership of Iain Duncan Smith, it found a target for mockery which exceeded anything Labour could offer. Under Duncan Smith, the Conservative Party did modestly well – recovering in the polls, in mid-2003, to edge ahead of the government; winning over 600 council seats in the local elections of that year. Duncan Smith was not the equal of Tony Blair in either the heavily ritualized exchanges during prime minister's question time, nor in his ability to give direction and vision to his party. But he did articulate some promising themes for the Conservatives, especially on the European Union (a speech in Prague in July 2003 laid out competently, if with no great innovations, a moderate euroscepticism); on tax and personal responsibility; and on crime.

His cardinal weakness was, and was seen to be, his inability to appear well on the media. Thus what might have been a modest holding operation in leadership turned into a crisis-ridden period in which a reported £100,000 was spent in teaching him to walk decisively, greet supporters firmly and sincerely and project his voice and personality more forcefully. Not only did it not work: it had a largely perverse effect. From producing forced laughter on the 'Today' programme in response to questions about splits in his party and sackings in its administration, to the adoption of the 'quiet man' persona, he appeared as a man with a taste for grey suits forced to wear loud check several sizes too big for him. His media advisers – in whose sincerity in having his best interests at heart it's hard, in retrospect, to believe – produced a climax in his speech to the October 2003 Conservative Party conference, in which he shouted that 'the quiet man is here to stay and he's turning up the volume!'

Duncan Smith was a generally poor leader against whom several in his party – especially those round the disappointed would-be leaders Michael Portillo and David Davies – plotted almost as soon as his term of office began, after the 2001 general election. But he was the choice of the party in the country: not of the leading Tory MPs, and not, of course, of the media. Yet these two groups, in alliance, were the immediate cause of his early resignation.

It was here, in the ending of the term of office of a weak as against a strong leader, that the position of the media in democratic life is best tested. The argument made by journalists on Duncan Smith is that political journalists simply recognized, because of their proximity to power and their professional duty to judge politics and politicians, that Duncan Smith could not win long before Conservative activists, and certainly the mass of the electorate, could. It was their job – even duty – to say so. To present him positively – as the *Daily Telegraph* and the *Spectator*, mustering their reserves of loyalty still undrained by their desire to run with the media wolf pack, sporadically tried to do – would have been a distortion of reality.

This question is the best test, because the media rationale appears strongest: it has the power of the evident truth. But it is not evidently true for all media, and it is not evidently true if the media are to play the role which they claim to be their ultimate social and philosophical base: the underpinning of freedom and of democratic institutions. Neither of these goals is served by giving most space to the calls for removal of one who has been elected by members of his party a short time before; these can be expected to be given space in newspapers and journals opposed to the Conservatives. But any reasonable test of party loyalty, or of interest in pursuing politics on the right, would see these calls and plots relegated to a brief mention in favour of the discussion of policy, old and new, of the bases of opposition to Labour and Liberal Democrat; and to party organization.

A publicly funded broadcaster does not and cannot enjoy the ideological freedom of private newspapers. So it can't follow the wolf pack into the hunt. But it did. Duncan Smith's ill-judged 'ha ha ha' to John Humphrys' questions during a 'Today' programme interview was an attempt to fend off precisely the wolf-pack questions – which were the first ones to be asked in that interview. These had come to the top of the media agenda because they were on the top of the press agenda. But the scent of blood was too strong and exciting to be denied: the BBC had to be part of the chase.

The questions on Duncan Smith's ability to lead the Tory Party are not just legitimate: they are necessary. If, as was in the end the case, a large faction coalesced round an ultimately successful putsch against him, that had to be reported. But it was not reported – it was led. Few editors or commentators took the view – and none took it consistently – that what was important for the Conservative Party, and the country, was space devoted by the media to debate on and analyse the policies being promoted under Duncan Smith's leadership: Europe, immigration, crime, tax, public services. Even the issues seen as substantial and worthy of a lot of comment – such as his opposition to repealing legislation banning books 'promoting' homosexuality in schools – were cast merely in terms of inner-party rows, and little examined for their resonance with the electorate.

In an essay on populism, David Goodhart linked the power of the mass media to the lack of 'rootedness' in contemporary politics. He charted the change by noting that Stanley Baldwin, Conservative prime minister during the 1936 abdication crisis, told Tory MPs to go back to their constituencies and consult their local Conservative associations about whether or not Mrs Wallis Simpson, the king's mistress, should become the king's wife and thus queen. 'The idea,' wrote Goodhart, 'that John Major or Tony Blair would entrust a

105

great constitutional decision to their activists is laughable. It is now the reporters or the opinion pollsters who are sent out to discover what the people think . . . divided from each other in our actual neighbourhoods, we are virtually "re-connected" through the mass media.' But the media have gone a step further than finding out what the people think: they have replaced the politically active classes' judgements with their own – irrespective of what they, or the rest of the people, might think. And the public broadcaster plays no counterweighing role – on the contrary.

That was, above all, the BBC's job. The Conservatives under Duncan Smith were articulating a range of issues which were at the heart of national – and international – life. If Duncan Smith was not adept at speaking to all – or sometimes any – of them, they had a range of competent, at times brilliant, shadow ministers who could. Above all, they were the major party of opposition. Yet public service television, both that under a statutory duty to make some attempt to report news and current events, and the broadcaster funded by taxes raised on pain of legal action, mostly followed the press wolf pack. In his two and a half years of leadership, Iain Duncan Smith's policies and policy development attracted *not one serious programme of analysis and discussion from BBC television*. There was a great deal of discussion – on 'Today' and the other Radio 4 news magazine programmes, on 'Newsnight' on BBC 2 and elsewhere. But it was dominated by the presumed crisis in leadership; it was often confrontational; and it was never at length. There was a huge market failure: the private press was giving little space to explanation, analysis and discussion of policies, and doing little to test them against the electorate's wishes. The BBC was there to compensate for such market failure by running programmes which were serious explanations of Conservative (and other parties, such as the Liberal Democrats') policies. But it did very little to do so.

The sense of radical unfairness is common to both main parties. A conversation with the pollster Philip Gould early in 2004 revealed his and the government inner circle's sense of embattled frustration. He pulled out folders of charts, with opinion lines on the health service, on education, on crime – all going down over the years of the Labour governments since 1997, then turning up over the previous few months.

We're solidly ahead of the opposition on the economy. And in the last month or so (end of 2003/beginning of 2004) these have begun to tick up on most things – education, health service. People are beginning to see the results of the spending come through. But we're having the worst press we've ever had. We're supposed to be liars and bastards. The coverage bears no relation to reality.

I go to see the people at Downing Street quite regularly. I was with the prime minister yesterday, for a couple of hours. The people I see there are people like Jonathan Powell [the prime ministerial chief of staff], Sally Morgan [political secretary], David Hill [the press secretary, succeeding Alastair Campbell] and others. Gordon Brown, John Prescott. There's nothing special about what we say. If we were talking about the weapons of mass destruction [then the dominating issue in the media] people say: 'I don't know why they haven't found any. We thought Saddam had them.' But journalists think something else entirely goes on. As if there's quite another dialogue – secret, hidden, nothing to do with what is said publicly – instead of normal conversations much as you'd have anywhere.

I don't understand journalists. You are a world apart. I'll talk to a journalist and it will go perfectly well and everything seems to be understood – and then what comes out is unrecognizable. It's not political opposition or rational criticism – who could object to that? It's just removed from reality. Journalists are removed from reality. I

107

try not to get involved. I have my relationship with the prime minister and his people and then I go out and do my focus groups and find out what people are thinking.

I think now that people think some things because of their experience and other things because of the media. There was a woman in one focus group some years ago, when we were asking about the Dome [the exhibition-cum-theme park in Greenwich, built as a tribute to the millennium, which failed to attract the anticipated crowds]. She said, 'I went along with the kids: we quite enjoyed it.' Then she stopped, looked round, and said something like, 'Of course, that was before I knew it was a disaster!' She had realized that she'd said something which wasn't the media version of events, that everyone else was saying. So people will say that the National Health Service is a disaster and the local hospital is really good.

In a conversation I'd had with a senior government information officer, I had some confirmation of that approach. Like others, this officer lived in fear that the *Mail* or another paper would explode a horror story under their minister; their aim, I was told, is 'not to get stories in – we've stopped doing that – but just to keep them out'. As a broadcast journalist before government service (not for the BBC), the officer had been sent out with the order to 'get a bad story on the National Health Service' – preferably in the prime minister's constituency, or that of the then health secretary, Alan Milburn. The story had been got – but only, the officer told me, at the price of a clear distortion of the facts. Most responses had been positive. 'I found, in the end, a senior nurse ready to talk, with a complaint about some supplies in the hospital where she worked.' Thus in the report, a particular incident could be taken to represent a more general crisis. This, the officer said, was one reason why government work had been more attractive: it had seemed a more worthwhile way to earn a living. TV – and especially the BBC – should be better. But it isn't.

TV current affairs in Britain are now largely on the BBC. Though Independent Television and more especially Channel 4 do documentaries and discussion programmes and of course have news bulletins, the programmes which distinguished them – such as 'World in Action', 'This Week', 'Weekend World' – have now gone, to be replaced with little. Jonathan Dimbleby hosts a current affairs programme at midday on Sundays. The main current affairs series is 'Tonight', with Trevor McDonald; it is undemanding. Channel 4's hour-long news at 7.00 p.m. is a rare saving grace for the commercial sector.

The BBC, by contrast, has on its TV and radio channels the largest output of news and current affairs in the world – and, with BBC World (TV) and the BBC World Service (radio), it broadcasts around the world. It established itself as the world leader in broadcast journalism. When I did an interview about the BBC for the German (state) TV station ZDF, the programme – a nightly, 7.30 programme on culture – began with a short clip in which the commentator pointed out that the BBC had been, for post-war Germany, a model to be emulated. This model now, sadly (the German word *schadenfreude* came to mind here) had because of the Kelly affair been called into question. The station's writers might have reflected before the Kelly affair that no mainline BBC TV channel would dream of having a 7.30 p.m. programme on culture: who was being a model to whom?

Greg Dyke, the BBC director general from 1999 to his forced resignation in 2004, cut back hard on the news. He pushed 'Panorama' out to a late slot on Sunday evenings, put the news on at 10.00 in the evening, killed the analytical Sunday politics programme 'On the Record' and all but destroyed arts

109

programming. Two weeks before the Hutton Report appeared, Dyke and Richard Sambrook, head of BBC News, submitted themselves to an extraordinary internal quizzing before some 300 of their colleagues on the affair (which Dyke then thought he would weather) by the newspaperman turned TV presenter Andrew Neil and the BBC World ('Hard Talk') interviewer Tim Sebastian. At one point, Neil observed to Dyke that, in the first week of the year, the entire BBC output on the arts had been half an hour; by contrast, it had covered championship darts for 40 hours. Dyke, seeing a jokey opportunity in what was otherwise a harsh interview, said, 'Well . . . I'm an insomniac and I like watching darts in the middle of the night' – a small pretence that the BBC was a personal entertainment machine.

But he wasn't really a populist: he was a TV executive in an age of popular programming who wasn't John Birt. Birt, who became as unpopular with large sections of the BBC staff as Dyke became popular, was easily caricatured as a humourless dictator. One former 'Panorama' producer, the author Tom Bower, wrote of him as a Stalin, whose 'Stalinists' imposed a 'year zero' of frozen banality on such programmes as 'Panorama' which, when Bower had been part of its team (until 1987 – the year Birt arrived at the BBC as deputy director general) had been 'a programme of passion, pride and principle for which lives were risked and marriages destroyed to produce unwelcome but irrefutable truths'.

Birt had done many zany things in his rapid rise through the ranks of Granada in the late 1960s and early 1970s when the Manchester-based independent TV station was the most adventurous pro-gramme maker, perhaps (at the time) in the world, under the left-wing entrepreneur Sidney Bernstein. Above all he did *noticeable* things – most famously, having Mick Jagger explain his incoherent radicalism to an Archbishop of Canterbury, a former home secre-tary and an editor of *The Times* in the open air. But he wanted to understand the world and to share the understanding with others. He thus created 'Weekend World' for London Weekend TV – an hour-long programme which became famous for its careful explanatory style and for its courteously forensic interviews conducted by its main presenters – in turn, the economic journalist Peter Jay, and the former MPs Brian Walden and Matthew Parris. With Jay, Birt had written two articles for *The Times* which became known as the 'Bias against Understanding' case: arguing that TV news and current affairs gave in to the temptation to follow the pictures, not tell the story; and that thus TV viewers were not being given an adequate account of the world – 'this bias aggravates the difficulties which our society suffers in solving its problems and reconciling its difficulties'.

It was an analysis which appealed and continues to appeal to those who were searching for a way of preserving public service journalism. Some of these were also upset by the callow radicalism of much of what was offered as current affairs – including from Birt's old programme, Granada's 'World in Action', which he had co-edited with the Labour minister-to-be, Gus Macdonald. Birt became deputy, then in 1992 director general, of the BBC in part because he was seen as a man who would 'save' it. He thought its news and current affairs operations at best patchy; its journalists too 'willing to offer their own opinions rather than undertaking rigorous, open-minded explorations of all sides of the issue'. When making calls on Prime Minister Margaret Thatcher and opposition leader Neil Kinnock, he learned that both thought the BBC lacked quality, management talent and efficiency. In a conversation with Thatcher, he heard her say that 'Marxism is at the root of debunking journalism', to which he responded that:

> much journalism assumed that a problem identified was a problem for the state to solve. I argued that there were other powerful

111

influences on our national culture: disputation – undermining your opponent's case – was at the heart of our parliamentary, debating and judicial systems. The anarchist tendency, exemplified by *Private Eye* and its renegade public schoolboys, enjoyed throwing everything up in the air. And the self-confident Oxbridge tradition of we-know-best commenting was a literary rather than an analytical tradition. There were many reasons why British journalism did not grapple with Britain's problems.

Birt's belief that the BBC journalists had a tendency to prefer the dramatic to the analytical, action pictures to coherence, disjointed commentary to coherent narrative, did not, of course, go down well with most of them. A few – such as 'Panorama' reporter John Ware (who was to do a fine report on the Kelly affair), the producers Tony Hall, Mark Byford, Tim Gardam and Mark Damazer who rose under him – became convinced of some or much of his argument. But the culture did not change fundamentally. Birt thought that the increasingly abrasive interviewing style – displayed most notably by John Humphrys on the 'Today' programme and Jeremy Paxman on 'Newsnight', the news shows that began and ended the day – drew heat, but shed no light. Yet these two figures were untouchable and untouched. He tried to cut against the culture, by hiring high-level specialists; and he did raise the tone and seriousness of the main news bulletins. In Ian Hargreaves, his head of news and current affairs from 1987 to 1990, he had a journalist of the same evangelically analytical persuasion as he was. Birt brought over from London Weekend a slew of people – Glenwyn Benson, Samir Shah, David Jordan, David Aaronovitch – who ran departments and programmes which reflected his approach. But he felt he only partly succeeded in his core mission. In a speech he gave in Dublin in 1995 – only three years after his appointment to the

112

top job – he re-stated his credo: that politicians came before journalists, politics before journalism.

> Some journalists, sometimes, forget that. Reporters who pretend that answers and remedies are obvious; that everyone in the world but themselves is an incompetent fool; overbearing interviewers who sneer disdainfully at their interviewees; the sub who composes a crass and unfair headline; the columnist at his or her desk pontificating angrily – all exhibit attitudes which are unattractive in a journalist and rarely appropriate.

The speech caused a huge commotion inside the BBC: most of the journalists rallied round the stars and accepted the view of Birt as an establishment hack; his supporters thought the speech made the slow patient work of changing attitudes impossible – and was a recognition that Birt had already come to that conclusion. In the last three or four years of his leadership, the gains were minimal. He made the BBC a much more serious and better run place. His lobbying, and his record, secured it very large licence fee increases. He backed his journalists on difficult stories – as the world affairs editor John Simpson recognized when under political pressure while reporting from Belgrade. He had brought in specialists to, and raised the culture of, the news. But much of current affairs didn't change fundamentally.

In 2002 at a party held to commemorate the 25 years since the founding of 'Weekend World', Matthew Parris – the third of the three 'Weekend World' presenters – gave a little speech in which he said that the programme which Birt had created, had been a brave experiment and that he had not done it justice, being the least effective of the three presenters (which was true). But he thought perhaps the project had been doomed. TV simply didn't accommodate that kind of analytical rigour. It was a thought left hanging in the air of a largely self-congratulatory gathering. But it is an important question.

Birt, from his entry to the BBC, was cutting against its grain. It had been a loose set of fiefdoms: its news division was often insular; it could develop a poisonous atmosphere of intrigue and backbiting which in turn produced a conformism in all but brave or very ambitious souls. It was as leftist as an institution whose journalists were largely middle-class arts graduates would be expected to be – but who did not, or did not often, examine their own bias, or think they expressed one.

James Purnell, now a Labour MP, was a BBC policy planner from the mid-1990s and then an adviser on broadcasting in the Downing Street policy unit. Over coffee in the new MPs' building opposite Westminster, he told me that 'when Birt came he believed that the BBC newsroom had a "pack" mentality: it ran after stories others did. He did change the news but "Panorama" and "Newsnight" stayed out of the change.' So, in a different way, did the 'Today' programme – especially under Rod Liddle, its editor from 1998 to 2003, and Kevin Marsh, the present editor. Birt had never seen it as the enemy he saw at 'Panorama' and 'Newsnight', but he did often scold it for unfairness to politicians, one of his constant preoccupations.

Birt believed he was fighting ingrained, snobbish, anti-politician attitudes – the kind he had talked about to Mrs Thatcher – much as Blair fought Old Labour. He was losing against these attitudes: they prevailed and deepened. But he was also fighting, and largely losing to, media trends that have had a profound effect on contemporary news and current affairs, and which were way beyond his control.

All of British public life has grown much more open and harshly questioning over the last two decades. In part this is a reflection of the well-discussed decline in public manners and deference, which politicians find unnerving – though in which many continue to indulge, or to acquiesce, when in opposition. Peter Mandelson has twice been forced from cabinet office by revelations in the media – first of a secret arrangement to borrow money from a fellow Labour MP to buy a house and failure to declare the loan on a mortgage application form; then of discreet pressure on a fellows minister to obtain a British passport for a Labour Party donor. In his rooms in the Commons, he told me:

> Everyone is now treated in the same way: politicians, celebrities, sports people, without discrimination. The standards of manners and courtesy have dropped. There's a lack of any kind of respect for achievement and status. There is no feeling for what is private in life. Politicians, it seems, are regarded as being for the use of the media, purely and simply, to be used and abused.

The broadcaster has also – and unavoidably – succumbed to another dominant social influence of the last decade: celebrity culture. Since it commands audiences of millions, the BBC naturally produces stars, including news stars. Some, such as John Simpson, Kate Adie, Martin Bell, Jeremy Paxman, the Dimbleby brothers, John Humphrys, Andrew Marr, Fergal Keane, Martha Kearney, Rageh Omaar, Kirsty Wark and others, have or had very large followings because of their confident, intelligent and accessible broadcasting styles. Many, including Humphrys, Marr and Simpson, capitalize on their fame to write columns for newspapers and magazines. Rod Liddle was fired in 2003 for criticizing the Countryside Alliance movement in a column he wrote for the *Guardian*. In this context, the fact that Andrew Gilligan, ostensibly an objective BBC news reporter, wrote a column in the anti-government *Mail on Sunday*, did not appear terribly unusual – not even when he made his dramatic charge against Alastair Campbell, one not raised to him by BBC executives at the time.

Indeed, Gilligan was working within a culture of criticism of politicians – off-screen, as well as on. The BBC's top anchorman, Jeremy Paxman, has written contemptuously of the current political class. In his harshly dismissive (of politicians) 2002 book *The Political Animal*, Paxman stresses that parliament is now composed of yes-men and- women who have no independent judgement of their own. 'The picture of a parliament made up of people of autonomous mind, deciding what was best for the nation on the basis of personal judgement, belongs to the last century,' he wrote, adding, 'trivial people have become attracted to politics'. Humphrys, who professes to like politicians, is certain that since public meetings in which politicians are given a hard time no longer attract audiences, and since people don't check on parliamentary business, 'it is largely on television and radio that real probing of what politicians are up to has to happen' – an enormous assumption of journalism's primacy in the political process.

When Greg Dyke replaced Birt as director general of the BBC in 1999, the two were, ostensibly, friends. They were the two leading products of London Weekend's current affairs department – Dyke had been hired as a researcher in the London Weekend TV current affairs department when Birt headed it in the mid- to-late 1970s. They shared an attachment to the Labour Party, especially to New Labour – which they saw as a necessary political project. In Birt's memoir, *The Harder Path*, they are shown in a photograph as lads together, in football gear, in 1999.

But the two were quite different. Dyke, though he had begun in current affairs, soon shifted to the show business side of TV, then moved up quickly to manage divisions, then companies (including the TV division at Pearson, the owners of the *Financial Times*, which furnished him with glowing references when he applied to the BBC). In the process, he became rich. He was unlikely to be Birt's choice as his successor, though the latter did not make a recommendation – commenting only in his memoir that, in his first interview, Dyke had 'by common consent, been unconvincing on the public service rationale of the BBC, uncomfortable with the BBC's higher purpose'.

Dyke, in office, could at times both defend and promote testing current affairs programmes. As head of the BBC, Dyke was a guardian of public service broadcasting and has spoken for it in many forums – including, with pride, in the United Nations. But he has indeed not communed with its higher purpose in the same way as Birt. Birt believed, and came to believe with greater and greater fervour, that the BBC had a 'mission to explain'; he did not much care if BBC 1, the main channel, was regularly beaten by ITV – as it was. Dyke at times seemed to want to believe in the higher purpose, but he also believed that only if the BBC was popular could it remain publicly funded. And he made it so: its programmes were usually ahead of all the competition from the other terrestrial, and from cable and satellite, channels in the top ten list.

He has been impatient with news and current affairs – not usually, as Birt was, for bias or lack of rigour, but for not getting an audience. And if he did not bewail the lack of current affairs' pulling power, the channel controllers he had appointed to run BBC 1 and BBC 2 – Lorraine Heggessy and Jane Root – certainly did. They would show him graphs where viewer figures – which can now be measured minute by minute – dropped as off a cliff once a current affairs programme followed a popular soap or game show. He felt their pain and, in the main, let them off the leash. Dyke wanted a new show called 'If . . .', which would test hypotheses for the future based on present trends (and which ran in the Spring of 2004); he had to fight Root through meeting after meeting to get her to accept it. In the Department of Culture, Media and Sport and in the newly created regulator Ofcom, ministers and officials blamed Dyke for letting the channel controllers have the last say on what current affairs programmes they would take, and what kind of news content they preferred – although even before he made this switch, the controllers could put up a formidable block to anything they didn't want. But he was in practise closer to the position taken on news by Rupert Murdoch of News Corporation – whom he had for many years disliked – than he was to Birt's. For Murdoch, news is a business like any other: standards, balance and fairness are something the market can take care of. For Dyke, ratings and audience levels are a very large part of what he thinks news and current affairs should be about – and his BBC sought to get higher ratings for fewer current affairs programmes in a way it did not under Birt.

He called himself a news junky, but he liked his news to be as combative, irreverent and bull-headed as he could be. He did not have, or certainly did not articulate, the kind of sophisticated critique of news output which Birt had to Margaret Thatcher. He was a TV businessman; Birt, a TV intellectual. He did not fret about the news, or its bias: he let the editors, producers and reporters get on with it. He spent a lot of time on re-organizing the management systems – or rather, shifting resources from management to programmes; flattening the hierarchy; and bringing back programme making to the BBC from the independent producers. Where Birt was seen as unapproachable and cold, ever apt to reach for a consultant or a new system, Dyke seemed enthusiastic, demotic and engaged. Birt turned outward, presenting a face to the world of a BBC which strove to be responsible, engaged in public debate, understanding of the problems of politicians and of government. Dyke turned inward, anxious to raise morale and get juices flowing, devolve power and make waves – and above all, beat the competition in the ratings. Both paid the price: Birt in the unpopularity with much of his news staff which came with challenging, or scorning, their journalism; Dyke, ultimately and more dramatically, with the political class.

In 2001–2, Dyke organized an internal review of news, which was spurred by BBC research department findings showing young people no longer watched the news and current affairs – 'young' being defined as up to the age of 40. He had seen the result of the 2001 election – that less than 60 per cent of the population had voted, and that young people in particular had stayed away from the polling stations in huge numbers – as a personal affront. He wanted to do something: to turn the country round through programmes which attracted the young to political life. The conclusion was that news had to become more populist, more chatty and more astringent; but few programmes flowed from it. One which did saw Rod Liddle, who had edited the radio show 'Today', brought back to do a populist and astringent news political programme on Saturday morning. It didn't work, and was killed after six episodes.

Dyke's changes went with the grain; indeed, in TV circles, they had the air of inevitability. Working with his director of television Mark Thompson (who later became head of Channel 4), Dyke carved a swathe through BBC 'high-mindedness', bearing the standard of the people's right to choose. The classic statement of this is in a speech which not he, but Thompson, gave at the annual TV festival in Banff, Canada. Mocking those who wished to retain the current shape of the commitment to public service TV as struck in a past in which choice was limited, Thompson protested that he was among those who believed that 'public broadcasters around the world do need to act to protect seriousness and creative diversity, and to do it boldly and with fresh ideas'. Thompson set the modern broadcaster in a new universe – one in which there had been an 'explosion of choice' through digital and satellite channels. The research the BBC had done into the homes with this new choice showed that a fast-growing number used the electronic programme guide (EPG) to zap about the new universe. The old

idea of 'hammocking' – putting current affairs and arts programmes between popular favourites in the belief that people
wouldn't switch off or over – didn't work any more. 'You can,'
said Thompson, 'study the charts of 15-second audience movements and see them go the moment they realize that a given
programme doesn't meet their mood or expectations.'

Elite culture, of the kind hammocked between popular shows,
was 'just one more niche which appeals to a diminishing minority'.
In its place, he suggested, should be programmes which run with
the flow of what was already being created – the disappearance of
the 'serene, knowable middle ground . . . and in its place, a
landscape of niches and categories'. Programming itself should
be niche: the 'big' channels, such as BBC 1 and 2, should be given
over largely to popular entertainment, with 'an entire digital
channel [devoted] to serious music and the arts, and to the world
of ideas in science, politics and philosophy'. Thompson and Dyke's
niche vision was followed through. BBC 1 and 2 lost nearly all of
what had remained of classical music and arts programming and a
good deal of current affairs. BBC 4 was created, with much the
'niche' brief which Thompson had outlined in Banff. So was BBC 3,
a channel aimed at youth.

At their back, Dyke, Thompson and the others in the BBC who
became convinced that they were right, heard the winged chariots
of Rupert Murdoch. Dyke half-admired, half-detested Murdoch;
the two had been head-to-head in a battle over Murdoch's Sky
TV's – ultimately successful – efforts to take the rights for premier-
ship football. When Murdoch gave the MacTaggart Lecture at the
Edinburgh TV Festival in 1990, in which he said that British TV
was in the grip of a self-serving Oxbridge elite, Dyke, then con-
troller of programmes at London Weekend and a growing force in
the TV industry, took it personally: 'It's quite flattering to think
that anyone could describe me as part of an elite who doesn't give a

toss about what the public wants, and that I run it just for my own gratification'. Dyke was right to feel a bit put out by Murdoch's blanket assumption that no one in the British media understood the way the world was going but him. Unlike many in British broadcasting, and unlike almost everyone in the BBC, Dyke saw early what was happening to television. It was losing its licence to know what was good for the audience. He was saying to Murdoch: I'm on your side.

Murdoch's side has become increasingly easy to define in the past decade. He stands for the market – in news, as in everything else. If people want news, he thought, they should have news; as much, or as little, as they want – and of whatever bias they like. In May 2003, Murdoch appeared at a US Senate Committee hearing on changes of the rules which restricted the number of TV and radio stations one person or corporation may own (the rule change went through the Federal Communications Commission, FCC, later in the year, leaving corporations much freer in their business activities). Asked by the Democrat senator from North Dakota, Byron Dorgan, about the imbalance of political views on talk radio and TV – to the tune of 300-plus hours of nationally syndicated conservative talk each week as against five hours of liberal talk – Murdoch said, 'Apparently conservative talk is more popular', adding: 'if we could find a popular, amusing liberal broadcaster to talk for an hour or two every day then we'd have him on like a shot.'

In his sponsorship of Fox TV – which is now surpassing CNN in the ratings – and in his talk radio stations, Murdoch is pioneering, or bringing back, openly biased media. The notion of objectivity in journalism – and the concomitant notion of journalism as a public service for citizens – has had a flickering life for centuries, but only took proper shape and became an influential, even dominant, mode in the nineteenth century, with godfathers as diverse as the US newspaper tycoon Joseph Pulitzer, the US news magazines and the BBC (it was always largely Anglo-Saxon in conception and execution). One hundred years ago, Joseph Pulitzer – whose papers sometimes did not live up to his ideals – produced an orotund saying on his profession: 'Our republic and its press will rise or fall together. A cynical, mercenary demagogic press will produce in time a people as base as itself.' The phrase is now engraved in the entrance to Columbia University's journalism school. Like the UK and other rich states, the US required that TV serve the public good through the provision of news and current affairs programmes. The chairman of the FCC in the Kennedy administration, Newton Minnow, told the National Association of Broadcasters in 1961 that their programmes amounted to a 'vast wasteland' and that 'I am here to uphold and protect the public interest. Some hold that the public interest is merely what interests the public: I disagree.' Since the 1980s, however, successive US governments have largely agreed that, in the words of Ronald Reagan's choice as chairman of the FCC, Mark Fowler, TV was only a 'toaster with pictures': that is, it needed only the lightest of technical controls, and otherwise was a commodity like sliced bread.

Murdoch has been, as ever, the clearest sighted on what the progressive lifting of controls has meant: freedom from objectivity, freedom to air increasingly raucous opinions. James Fallows, in a lengthy piece of reflective reporting on Murdoch and his effect on broadcasting, draws an important conclusion.

Fox TV . . . covers news – sort of. Like its cable TV competitors, it really covers whatever is most attention getting that day. If it's a war, there is very interesting coverage of that war. If there's no war, then there's almost equally intense coverage of . . . whatever is compulsively watchable at the moment. The old-fashioned concept of news involved some sort of calculation of what was 'important'.

122

News as a pure business has to go with what grabs attention and hope that from time to time it's important too . . . an age of more purely commerical, more openly partisan media leaves out some of the functions that news was until recently expected to perform: giving a broad public some common source of information for making political decisions, and telling people about trends and events they didn't already know they were interested in. One way or another, self-governing societies must figure out the suitable commercial channels through which the information necessary for democratic decisions must be spread. That's not exactly Rupert Murdoch's problem, though he helped make it the world's.

Whoever must deal with this problem, it is increasing. The state, everywhere, had been able to make a deal with broadcasters: that is, in exchange for a license to broadcast (which generally *has* been a license to print money), it demanded a certain amount of civic television – news, current affairs, arts, information, community programmes, education. It was able to do that because it monopolized the electromagnetic spectrum, on which only a limited number of channels could co-exist.

Broadcast TV is still by far the most watched: the broadcast channels had had many years to establish dominance; they have much more money; they have the mainstream programmes; and they are easy to find. But satellite and digital channels are growing very rapidly: some 90 per cent of UK households are likely to have them by 2010.

The problem with Birt was that he created too few Birtists: or at least, none prepared to argue his case as passionately as he did. His lecture to Mrs Thatcher on the causes of the faults in British journalism was something in which he had come to believe more deeply than anything else in his professional life; and of course, it put him at odds with most journalists, since they usually had one or other version of these faults. Further, he was vulnerable: he had done little reporting, and had done almost no foreign reporting, absolutely no war reporting. Foreign, and above all war, reporting was a measure of journalistic credibility for the BBC, even more than it is elsewhere in journalism. To risk one's life and limb in the cause of TV images was seen, with some reason, as being the most obviously extreme commitment one could make to the cause of public service journalism. The men and women who did this journalism often became famous: of the now middle-aged generation, Kate Adie, Martin Bell and John Simpson all became household names and faces in large part through putting themselves at risk – and, in the latter two cases, sustaining injuries in doing so. What injuries had Birt sustained? What doors had he put his foot in? How many warplanes had he counted out and counted back in? There are few hauteurs higher than foreign reporters' disdain for those who have not shared their craft.

Yet Birt challenged, and angrily challenged, and *publicly* (outside the BBC) challenged BBC journalism. For him, journalism was only really serving the public if it made everything logical and clear. He was a rationalist: the world could and must be explained through discovering a narrative – both a story line for any given programme, or indeed any given interview, which went from A to C through B and was clearly intelligible to the careful listener/viewer; and a deeper narrative, which discovered through analysis and discussion what the political or social momentum of the times was. He thought he and his London Weekend colleagues were able to tell both stories, but that the BBC was in the position of the 'Mr Jones' in the Bob Dylan song, where 'something was happenin'/But you don't know what it is'. Birt's biggest gripe against the BBC was that it got Margaret Thatcher wrong: he wrote that 'the BBC had not yet come to terms with Thatcher. For ten years or more, LWT had been in the thick of the political and economic debate about what was wrong with Britain. The BBC's journalism, on the other hand, was still trapped in the old post-war Butskellite, Keynesian consensus. Many BBC people found it hard to think of Mrs Thatcher as democratically legitimate, perceiving her as an aberration.'

After Birt, such notions as the larger narrative largely faded from view, together with the higher purpose. It was not that no one thought them: it was that there was little point in thinking them. No programme would contain them. That was not just the fault of Greg Dyke – though he certainly showed little interest in such things. It was more that TV itself had changed, to some degree in synchronization with the press.

The victim of this mindset has been a current affairs coverage which – in the words of the BBC Charter – must be 'comprehensive, authoritative and impartial'. It is impartial in an important respect: as among the various parties, in the words of the report, *Bias and the BBC?* from a right-of-centre think-tank close to the Conservative Party's modernizers: 'apart from some isolated incidents, the BBC appears to give fair coverage to the Conservative Party. It is generally conscious of the need to allow both parties to present their cases. Insofar as the Liberal Democrats have obtained a larger share of the vote and a larger number of MPs, it is also fair that they be given a larger share of airtime, and here too the BBC meets its obligations.'

But party balance is always only a part of the obligation to be impartial. Where parties were clearly ideologically distinct, the balance was crucial – and easier. The two or three or more political philosophies needed to have equal force granted to them. But parties of the left- and right-of-centre are not so clearly distinct. Their cases are sometimes close, even the same. They believe roughly the same things about the economy; about retention of a nuclear deterrent; about the system of alliances; about the retention of state education and health services as the major provision for most people. The two main parties agreed about the need to invade Iraq. For some years, the major – and important – division between them has been on the European Union and (presently) the desirability of sterling being renounced in favour of the Euro.

Broadcasters have reacted to this by acting as an opposition, not so much to one party or the other, but to government: even, to politics. They have done this in three ways: by becoming openly abrasive and cynical; by assuming the position of the opposition; and by making little or no examination of the deeper biases than the purely party political.

The central claim is that – since the official opposition is weak, or (as John Humphrys claims) interest in parliament and political meetings is low – broadcasters must carry the burden of posing the hard questions and making the dispassionate analysis. The position is hugely self-serving – it promotes the media, and especially BBC journalism, to the status of an elected body, when in fact the latter is dependent upon the votes of elected representatives for its existence. It exists with a pervasive, if amused and matey, dismissal of politicians – especially those who challenge the broadcasters. In his memoir on his time at the BBC, Will Wyatt, who rose to just below the top of the TV hierarchy to retire as Dyke came in, tells of a time when he had to go before the Select Committee on Culture and Sport of the House of Commons to explain why the BBC was about to drop 'Yesterday in Parliament', the half hour between 8.30 and 9.00 a.m. devoted to selections from the previous day's debates in the Commons. He wrote that its chairman, Gerald Kaufman, 'seized the opportunity to grandstand on this' – asking Wyatt to give assurances that the BBC would not drop the programme until the committee had reported to the House. Wyatt said he and his colleagues had consulted for seven months and spoken to 100 MPs. Wyatt describes the reaction: 'Kaufman then inflated himself like a puffing frog. "This is the select committee of the House of Commons. This is not an informal group or one-to-one consultation over lunches or drinks or in some other way. This is the Select Committee on Culture and Sport of the House of Commons whose duty it is to make report to the House of Commons." ' Wyatt, a man of some sensitivity (at least as represented in his own words) was nevertheless imbued with the same arrogance as others of his, class of 1965, generation. He regarded Kaufman as a bit of a freak. Any politician who insisted on the privileges of parliament over those of the media was bound to look, to a senior BBC executive at the end of the twentieth century, like a 'puffing frog'.

This is the most important area of all: for it speaks to the broadcaster's inability to ingest and reflect and produces a new approach for an age in which politics itself is in flux. Politics is, and has been for some time, in radical flux. Left and right categories don't contain much any longer: in Anthony Giddens' phrase, we are 'beyond' them. On the part of the media, this has tended to result in an agreement that all governments are equally open to attack by everyone, a view which has penetrated deep into the broadcasting establishment. A formal left-right balance – or balance between and among the parties – remains. But for an understanding of politics, it is a long way from being sufficient.

The right-of-centre think-tank report acknowledged that the BBC was fair and balanced in its election-time mode, and in giving spokesmen and women from the main parties time on air roughly proportionate to their vote. But it also did an analysis of the BBC's current affairs stance through its most important programme, 'Panorama'. That found that the programme had a leftish bias, fairly consistently. It found what it identified as howlers – as commentary which posed as opposite free markets and high levels of employment; which assumed that a free market in housing created 'more losers than winners'; and calls for much tougher consumer protection without mentioning the costs. All these were evidence, said the report, of 'the BBC's institutionally left-of-centre nature of BBC political and current affairs coverage'.

There is something to this; indeed, it would be surprising if there were not. The BBC employs, largely, arts graduates as its editorial staff (John Birt's possession of an engineering degree was a constant subject of comment in writings about the BBC). These are, in the UK, very largely on the left politically – sometimes moderately, sometimes radically. Current affairs journalism has generally had a strong radical tinge: Granada's 'World in Action', one of the alma maters of John Birt, was a leader in this. Thus – as an index of the state of affairs – while it is easy to believe that a programme on the housing market which found more losers than winners would be made, it would be unlikely that a programme would be made exposing the 'scandal' that a stable majority in most European countries wanted the return of capital punishment – but were denied their wish by parliamentarians who would not sanction a return to the practise. The choice of what is worth investigating is as much a pointer to bias as the way in which it is investigated.

When Dyke first came to the BBC, he also thought it had a bias to the left – specifically in one area, that of business coverage. Dyke had become rich in the TV business; he had also been for some months in 1989–90 to Harvard Business School, after which – according to his biographers – 'he would say that at Harvard he had glimpsed the real nature of competition in business and the degree of ruthlessness that was needed to succeed'. He was interested in business, in both its strategy and details, and he found the BBC's coverage dismal. In a speech to the CBI in November 2000, he said, 'I don't think that the coverage of business on radio and television over these [past] two decades has been good enough.' Generalizing from his own experience, he said, 'There has been a huge increase in the number of people with a direct financial interest in business prosperity and an even bigger increase in people who want to understand what is going on and why.' Instancing a recent running story on the management buyout of the car company Rover, he said, 'we even dragged Red Robbo [the union convenor Derek Robinson, known for his militancy at the then British Leyland in the 1970s and 1980s] out of retirement for a comment' – implying, as one producer said afterwards, 'that we were all a bunch of lefties'. The producer was right: Dyke did think that. In a throwaway comment after the speech, Dyke joked with the delegates: 'We're all capitalists now'. He did not comment – it was a worried theme among business journalists a year or two later, as Richard Lambert, former editor of the *Financial Times*, commented self-critically – on how many very large financial and corporate scandals his business coverage was missing.

He brought in as business editor – a new post, equal in status to political, economics and foreign affairs editor – Jeff Randall, a former business journalist on the *Sunday Times* and *Sunday Business* (of which he had been editor). Randall told me that in his talks with Dyke, the two had agreed that the news and current affairs people were infected with a knee-jerk sense that all business was suspect, all mergers or takeovers had to be seen solely through the prism of layoffs and all profits were too high, except when they were losses, which could then be called a crisis.

Mark Damazer, the deputy director of news, part of whose job is to absorb the various news policy demands on the BBC, told me that though much had changed on the coverage of business, much more still had to. Damazer had himself done a secondment to a US business school, in his case to Wharton.

You begin to appreciate issues that you had not before. For example, that retrained earnings is a sign of health, a necessity for a company. But did we say this on our coverage on BT? I think we were right to stress its monopoly position and to ask about the remuneration of its top executives. But did we understand enough that it needed to make a huge profit in order to compete as a global company in the telecom market? Did we think, even, that its apparently gigantic profit might be too small for what it is setting out to do?

Damazer may have been converted to the benign possibilities of a large profit; others were obviously not. In a 'Today' programme in February 2004, Randall was brought on to do a two-way interview with presenter Edward Stourton on the large profits just announced by the Royal Bank of Scotland. The contrast in accents was quite marked: Stourton has a smooth, upper-Home Counties accent, Randall a pronounced edge of lower-class London/south east in his voice. Randall explained why the profits were so great – because the bank had been lending a good deal at a time of low interest rates. Stourton put in, 'Profits? Some would say profiteering.' With a slight pause, Randall came back to say, with a further edge of irritation, 'Well, it would be disappointing if some people thought that . . .' and went on to explain, *à la* Damazer, the need for large profits to have large, world-beating British companies. This was less a comment on the Royal Bank of Scotland than a plain man's corrective to Stourton's upper-class populism, an exchange which explained Dyke's move to hire Randall in the first place. The conflicts within the BBC – struggles under the rug – are, to the experienced listener/viewer, often as entertaining and enlightening as the formal programmes.

Lacking Birt's severe framework, Dyke relied on his own preferences. He said as much to Will Wyatt, then director of television, when he joined: he found the BBC, he told Wyatt, 'very process driven . . . I like to rely on instinct.' News, under him, was left much more to its own devices. It adopted a different kind of approach to business because the director general said it had to. It threw bones to powerful lobbies – such as the Countryside Alliance, or Business for Sterling, both lobbies identified more with the right than the left – if they complained hard enough. But it didn't do and hasn't done what the times demand – a thorough going, and at least partly public, examination of how news and current affairs should be produced by a publicly-funded broadcaster.

The battles over news and current affairs took place in a media context which affected them profoundly. At the same time as Birt was trying to push the BBC in the direction of more news, analysis and explanation of the world, the deeper trend in entertainment TV was encouraging what might be termed an 'anti-current affairs' mentality. Social analysis and public interest revelation, which once got the critical kudos, were being shifted aside in favour of a new form: self-analysis and personal revelation. The programme which illustrated this better than any other was the extraordinarily successful 'Big Brother' – developed in the Netherlands by a company called Endemol – and its British producer, Peter Bazalgette.

Bazalgette discovered the fascination of the ordinary act, and the ordinary relationship, observed. When he gave the 2001 Wheldon Lecture (named after the famously high-minded BBC arts programme presenter, Huw Wheldon) he described why his kind of TV was so popular: 'This is a tolerant generation,' he said. ' "Big Brother" became a celebration of this generation's attitudes. As TV gets closer to the bone, the more honest, the more real, the better it is.' Reality, on this definition, was simple doing: without a point, except its own interest.

Barry Cox, who had been a director of London Weekend TV (with John Birt) and became deputy chairman of Channel 4, says: 'Peter Bazalgette is the key to the late 1980s–1990s television. He grasped that in TV programmes, to make people happy, you must set things up so there's a positive ending – which current affairs doesn't do. Bazalgette went into the home, and into personality and character. Current affairs had stayed with the issues.' The BBC has striven to make the intimate, populist style which Bazalgette brought to TV part of current affairs: a conscious leaching of entertainment techniques into news judgements.

This was not the invention of Dyke: it was well under way under Birt. Indeed, the comedy-fying-cum-demonising of politics on TV was a movement which came out of both the US counterculture of the 1960s and older satirical traditions found in most countries. They produced a burgeoning part of the entertainment industry which, in the hands of talented performers, could be very powerful. The harsh political comedy of the 1960s, however, went into abeyance; the left itself grew sanctimonious rather than comic. Only in the 1990s and 2000s has comedy/satire burst out once more as a political force, especially in the US: in writing, in films and TV shows, in standup acts. Books by Michael Moore, Al Francine, Molly Ivens and others have been huge bestsellers: nearly all have become so from representing President George W. Bush as a dangerous idiot. Moore, by far the most successful, came to wide notice by doing a film, *Roger and Me*, on layoffs from the General Motors plant in Flint, Michigan, where he had grown up and where his father had worked for GM. His fourth film, *Bowling for Columbine* (2002), on the shootings at Colombine High School, earned $212 million in the US, tripling the previous record for a documentary.

Nearly all of Moore's writings – *Downsize This!* (1996), *Stupid White Men* (2001) and *Dude, Where's My Country* (2003) – have been huge bestsellers worldwide. Moore is at least as popular in

132

Europe, including non-Anglophone Europe, as he is in the US. His success, as Larissa MacFarquar pointed out, is to get personal: no more abstract tirades against capitalism or imperialism, instead a steady focus on the figures in charge of whatever awful thing he is against – from Roger Smith, the chief executive officer of General Motors, in *Roger and Me* to George W. Bush in *Dude, Where's My Country*. MacFarquar makes a sharp point about Moore's (and his contemporaries') comedy: contrasting it with the comic protests of the 1960s–70s Yippies:

> To the Yippies, the world was ludicrous, America (or rather, Amerika) and its laws and customs were ludicrous, and the goal was to expose the absurdity so thoroughly that Americans would throw it all gloriously out of the window and start again . . . Moore doesn't find the world ludicrous and he doesn't want a revolution. When he talks about what America should be like, he talks about the good old days when people looked out for one another and stuck to old-fashioned values like the Golden Rule. Moore is a satirist and satire doesn't unseat conventions, it reinforces them.

This movement of political-personal absurdity, the belief – usually unstated – that today's politics and politicians are a travesty of those who were with us in the good old days, is one of the most powerful cultural currents of our times. Both of the most prominent presenters on BBC of the 1990s and 2000s, John Humphrys and Jeremy Paxman, tap that vein constantly – and almost subconsciously.

More openly, it informs much of the satiric comedy of the past few years. Most comedy that is not situation comedy would take a swipe at the government; some is extraordinarily critical – as is Rory Bremner, the mimic, whose programmes became, during the Iraq crisis, polemical attacks on members of the government, above all the prime minister. Blair was particularly in the firing line because of his alliance with, and support of, Bush and thus the British leader's intelligence could be held against him. Michael Moore, in a performance at the Cambridge Union in November last year, told the students that 'You're stuck with being connected to this country of mine, which is known for bringing sadness and misery to places around the globe. How's that feel? See, I actually hold Blair more responsible for this than Bush, because Bush is an idiot . . .'

Bremner, and the satiric talents of John Bird and John Fortune who often appear with him, are of course, put out under the heading of a joke: who but a humourless curmudgeon, or a politician, could object to that? But the effect has been to blur the edges between comment and wit and, because of the power of the medium, to imprint on millions of minds an image which – if it proves attractive – will stick to the public figure much more fiercely, and with much more effect, than the word or charges of a political opponent. Both British and American TV have blurred the edges between real and fictional politics by putting politics into dramas which portray as closely as possible the 'reality' of government. But the British do it more punitively. When 'The Deputy' – the British answer to the popular (in America) 'West Wing' – was unveiled on BBC 1 in February 2004, the *Sunday Times* wrote of it that:

the differences [with 'West Wing'] will be immediately apparent . . . [the Americans] had an Ivy League president who could play three games of chess simultaneously and still run the world; we get a guilt-ridden, overweight MP with a drink problem – 'a fat bastard'. The 'West Wing' was about a sexy, tight-knit group where everyone was likable. 'The Deputy' is about a paranoid bunch of back-stabbers who would sell their granny for political gain.

In the figure of 'Bob Galway', we got a caricature of the real deputy prime minister, John Prescott. The broadcaster, in televising a programme which shows Prescott in an extremely degrading light – he is treated with contempt by the fictional prime minister – is enabled to make a comment on real politics while relieved of the effort of doing a proper investigation which may or may not prove its point – and then being able to claim protection of fiction, or even fun. The programme, which portrayed politics as a hyper-cynical process in which the good can only be the victims of politics and politics can only squash the good, was a kind of apogee of the received view; it did, however, include the insight that the nightmare world which Galway inhabited had been largely constructed for him by the media and by fear of the media.

No politician could think of objecting – at least not publicly – to something which was 'only a joke'. But the effect of programmes such as 'The Deputy', or 'Spitting Image', or 'Bremner', are not jokes: they have real effects, perhaps very large effects, on political life. Lord David Steel, the former leader of the Liberal Party, believed that his portrayal in 'Spitting Image' of the 1980s as a fawning shadow of an imperious Dr David Owen, leader of the allied Social Democratic Party, cost the Liberal-Social Democratic Alliance the chance to displace Labour as the main party of opposition. Once again, choices made by electors were being very substantially altered by media; and because of the nature of the culture which assumed a right to intrude ever more decisively into what had been forbidden territory, not only was nothing being done about it, no serious questions were even being asked about it. Politicians became, in a variety of ways, more and more scorned and could barely object. The media would not allow it; it had been defined as a joke, millions of people liked it (they did) and thus its effects – whatever they are – cannot sensibly be discussed. The interest of the media – to attract as large a young audience as possible – takes advantage of the inherent British penchant for making a joke of serious matters.

*　　*　　*

The culture, pressures, mindset and leadership of the BBC came together, on 29 May 2003, at 06.07, to produce the broadcast two-way news interview between John Humphrys, the 'Today' presenter, and Andrew Gilligan over its claims about weapons of mass destruction (see transcript pages 3–4). Andrew Gilligan, who had a bent for pulling at the threads of stories until something came away and into the light, was again pulling on a promising thread. We know, because of the objections of the government which then led to the Hutton Inquiry, that the late David Kelly had told him an interesting story: he told much the same story to two other BBC journalists, Gavin Hewitt and Susan Watts. Both reflected some of the doubts which Kelly said existed in the intelligence services about the claim that missiles could be activated within 45 minutes – and about other issues on WMD – in broadcasts they made. These doubts had been aired before – notably in the *Observer*.

Indeed, the 45-minute claim was a thin one. It was shown to be almost certainly wrong and, months after the event, the prime minister said he had not known to which missiles the claim referred. Jack Straw, the foreign secretary, said neither he nor Tony Blair had attached much importance to the claim. Yet it was mentioned four times in the September dossier and had been given very large prominence – without apparent correction from government – in much of the tabloid coverage of the dossier. It was thus possible that what Gilligan said – that the prime minister knowingly lied – could have been true.

But that is what the story amounted to: some evidence; a suggestion; a possibility. On that edifice, a direct charge of prime ministerial lying was made. And it *was* a direct charge. A prime minister, especially one as hands-on as Blair is generally and certainly was during the Iraq war, always carries the can ultimately. The broadcast made sure that was known to be the case;

Humphrys personalized it: 'is Tony Blair saying they'd [WMD] be ready to go within 45 minutes?'

The 45-minute claim was, according to Gilligan, 'central' to the dossier. It was mentioned several times, but it wasn't central. It was a piece of evidence which was shockingly precise, hence its inclusion. But it wasn't central. Nor was the source who he said he was. He was not a senior official in charge of drawing up the dossier: David Kelly had contributed, as he later said, only a few lines.

Did Gilligan say that Blair – or the government – knew the 45-minute claim to be wrong? He said it twice, though the form of the broadcast was so shambolic – even given the informal standards of two-way broadcasts – that it allowed the BBC to later claim he had not. First, he said that 'the government probably knew that that 45-minute figure was wrong, even before it decided to put it in'. And again, at the end of the broadcast, when Humphrys had given an opening for Gilligan to play down what he had earlier said ('Does any of this matter now?'), he repeats it, apparently conditionally but actually unmistakably: 'things do, things are, got wrong in good faith, but if they knew it was wrong before they actually made the claim, that's perhaps a bit more serious.'

Gilligan's story was a lead: or, in the current British media environment, a tabloid story which, by its placing and treatment, implicitly asks to be taken with a pinch of salt – that is, it might be right, or it might be wrong, or it might be wholly made up. It was a promising lead: it was already placed in a context of stories reflecting doubts coming out of sources in the intelligence community (in one of the acid interchanges of letters between Richard Sambrook, head of news, and Alastair Campbell, the prime minister's director of communications, Sambrook uses the fact of the other news stories as proof that the Gilligan story had more than one source). So it was worth following; worth determining how the Joint Intelligence Committee was working; worth pointing to the tension in the intelligence services; worth illuminating the fact that John Scarlett, the chairman of the JIC and as such the senior adviser on intelligence, was working so closely with the prime ministerial aides, senior civil servants and ministers that they were – as the e-mail traffic divulged to Hutton shows – working at times as one team.

But the thread was not pulled: it was snapped, and presented to the public. And the most extraordinary thing about the story from the BBC's point of view, was Humphrys' question: '*Does any of this matter now?*'

Gilligan was broadcasting into, and out of, a culture which had been created through the interrelationships of many different forces, some of which have been described above. They produced, not his report – he did that – but an environment in which a reporter, ill-prepared, from his own flat, could charge the prime minister with a major, deliberate falsehood – and his interlocutor could at the end of it say: 'Does any of this matter?' It came from a programme whose previous editor had hired Gilligan because he was 'edgy': that is, he got anti-government stories. Gilligan's editor at the time of the broadcast, who took over from Rod Liddle, was Kevin Marsh, a more solid, careful, BBC man. His first instinct had been to defend the story – which he had shepherded on to air – unequivocally. In a memo to Stephen Mitchell, the head of BBC radio news, he wrote on 9 June: 'I started to look at this point by point and frankly it'd be easy to get as confused as [Alastair] Campbell is. The man is flapping in the wind . . . Downing Street has never explicitly denied the central charge . . . BBC journalists have been told . . . that the original story was correct.' In the same memo, Marsh writes – it was a consistent BBC delusion – that Gilligan had never accused the government of lying, but that 'we simply [said] that uncorroborated evidence was given prominence and that members of the security services were uncomfortable with that'.

A later memo from Marsh on Gilligan reads comically, especially when placed beside the earlier ones. On 27 June, as the heat began to come on the BBC and as various officials in the news division began to pull together a response, Marsh wrote, again to Mitchell: 'clearly I have to talk to AG early next week . . . the guts of what I would say are: this story was a good piece of investigative journalism marred by flawed reporting – our biggest millstone has been his loose use of language and lack of judgement in some of his phraseology'.

The memo is comic because of its internal contradiction. How can a piece of journalism of any kind be good if the reporting is flawed? What was Gilligan's journalism if not reporting? Marsh is doing the equivalent of a sports commentator claiming that 'it was a fine game marred by flawed football'. The statement, because of its clearly unconscious absurdity, comes from the same environment as the report itself, one which does not know what it is saying, indeed which got to the stage of claiming that words mean what the broadcasters say they mean. For weeks – months – the BBC denied it said what it said. Many in the BBC, and out of it, still do. Martin Kettle wrote in the *Guardian*:

> the episode illuminates a wider crisis in British journalism than the turmoil at the BBC; second, that too many journalists are in denial about this wider crisis; third, that journalists need to be at the forefront of trying to rectify it; and fourth, that this will almost certainly not happen . . . the more you read [the comment on the Hutton Report] the more you get the sense that the modern journalist is prone to behaving like a child, throwing its rattle out of the pram because it has not got what it wanted.

Gilligan's report should be set in stone at the entrance to the BBC, or at one end of Fleet Street, the former home of much of the British press. It is more useful to us in the media than any number of the quotations from Milton, Mill or Mencken which we roll out on occasions. It reminds us of what we have become. If the best of journalism – the BBC – could both put out a report like that and defend it, and remain (in many parts of the Corporation) convinced that it had been unfairly criticized by Hutton and traduced by government, then we have produced a media culture which in many ways contradicts the ideals to which we pay homage.

Greater Than Any of Them

MEDIA ARE at the centre of our public life. They define what that life is. If the definition they give of it is chronically, structurally wrong, then it's a serious matter, more serious than many of the things with which the media concern themselves. Media claim to have a central role to play in the construction and preservation of democratic life, liberty and the pursuit of happiness. Diverse views find expression through them – indeed, beyond a purely local existence, can do so *only* through them. Yet, outside the United States, media reflect relatively little on how they fulfill the central democratic purpose. It is usually assumed to be there, by virtue of the media's existence – so long as the state leaves them alone. Such a posture underestimates – either deliberately or unconsciously – the power of the media. It is because media wield such power, and that this is a power over society as well as a power to keep society free, that it's worth looking for ways for them to become more self-reflective and less careless with their power.

Anthony Sampson, who re-anatomized Britain early in 2004, wrote there that no sector increased its power (in the period between his first *Anatomy of Britain* in 1962, and the present) more than the media. 'Editors, journalists and cameras,' he wrote, 'penetrated nearly all institutions – including parliament, the monarchy, the political parties and Whitehall – demanding answers to irreverent questions, debunking their traditions and

141

clamouring for openness. They were not separate limbs or membranes in the anatomy so much as part of the lifeblood, or nervous system.' For all societies except those so underdeveloped that media hardly exist, the power of the media – sometimes the power of other people's media beamed in to poor states – is a large and growing political fact, with which politicians have to deal.

One of the media's proclaimed aims has always been truth. There are many others, which are less triumphantly proclaimed but which occupy more of the media's time, most of the time – as, for example, to entertain, to make a profit, to create celebrities. But telling the truth is journalism's Sunday best.

One of the ways we assume truth will emerge goes back to the method proposed in John Stuart Mill's *Essay on Liberty*, a work based on the assumption that from the clash of opinion, falsehood would be slain and truth appear. Mill did not, however, live to see how television deals with that proposition. In the clash of opinion, in the studios of 'Newsnight' and 'Today', the politician is invited in to be barked at. In the cauldrons of US television's 'Meet the Press' and 'McLaughlin's', the press people bark at each other, as well as at the politicians. In the theatrical-like expanses of Italian late night talk shows, politicians and other public figures dilate surrounded by pretty girls. On French and German TV, the tone is – or has been – more cerebral, but has increasingly tended to imitate the barking Anglo-Saxons, driven, in the German case, by a more aggressive press. In all these encounters, the audience in the studio and at home are implicitly, even at times explicitly, invited to judge not the issue but the performance. At times, TV and more often radio put on rational discussion, often in the wee hours, when only intellectuals are deemed to be awake.

The second Sunday-best suit is investigation; for that, the text is *All the President's Men*, the account in book and film, by the *Washington Post*'s Bob Woodward and Carl Bernstein, of the uncovering of the political corruption at the heart of the Nixon presidency. This was an important moment: that investigation, like others before and after it, brought measures of justice or redress and prompted reform. But this story can be beguiling: in bringing, in the recent cases, fame and celebrity to the journalists involved, they served as very powerful role models and do so still. This model can work to the public good, if the extraordinary care and labour which these two past reporters, and many other, journalists were enjoined to take by their own code of practise and by their editors, are followed. But it can be bad – in the BBC's case disastrous – when a small and perhaps questionable part of a larger narrative is mistaken for the revelation of a system assumed to be rotten.

It is beguiling because the model depends, not as in the Mill version on a clash of opinions, but on the overturning of stones. Turn over a stone, examine the insect life below and you have a revelation leading to a truth. But if the insect life is actually minding its own business in largely unsurprising ways, then the story tends to become the overturning of the stone itself. Truth can be on the surface, or more often, the hidden is only one part of the puzzle of what constitutes truth in any given issue.

There is a third kind of truth which can be sought through the media, which has become rarer almost everywhere. It is by explanation of contexts and events, using the rational tools of observation and inquiry. On a day-by-day basis, it is at least as essential to the maintenance of informed citizenship – which must be the largest reason to retain a publicly funded, ultimately state-controlled broadcaster such as the BBC. The market, we can assume on the basis of experience, can do entertainment. It cannot always do citizenship, at least not unaided.

The clash of opinion is necessary to inform democratic choice; so is the overturning of stones, for power and greed will always seek to disguise themselves. Rational inquiry and exposition is the necessary third leg, both necessary and more routine – the kind of work journalists are there to do, day after day, as medical staff are there to maintain health and teachers are there to transmit the culture and teach us how to think. Yet this third sort of truth-telling, which can often be the most precious, is less seen than it was. The passion to explain – what former director general of the BBC, John Birt, called the effort to counter the 'bias against understanding' which the reliance on image and spectacle makes inherent to TV – is attempted by only a few newspapers. It is barely offered at all on purely commercial TV channels. Public TV in every country is increasingly its last, certainly its largest, mass medium resort, but it is an increasingly squeezed one.

Journalists, who tell ourselves and others that we are an artery of democratic society, who have power of a kind and an extent we have never had before, can't duck the examination that power demands. That examination comes only partly from the daily 'referendum' which are readership and viewing figures. We wouldn't for a moment think that, in politics, mere popularity (and the popularity of the press is falling, almost everywhere) meant an end to examination because a given party had the sanction of voters; indeed, we'd assume it called for *more* examination.

Our own examination is crucially concerned with how the media tell the truth about society – about events, trends and public people. There must be some notion, common across journalism, of a reality which can be explained in a way that people of differing views, educational levels and backgrounds can agree is a reasonable representation. In this part of this essay, I want to try to give an account of what that could be. First, though, an impressionistic sketch of what truth has meant for us, in the media.

Théophraste Renaudot, who established a 'Bureau d'Addresses et de Correspondances' in seventeenth-century Paris under the protection of Louis XIII and Cardinal Richelieu, developed his fledgling postal service into an exchange for commodities, services and employment. In a leap of the imagination, he developed it further into a news exchange, by starting a gazette – whose first aim was to provide information for those seeking work. He had, he said, a 'passion for information'; he wrote: 'in one thing, I will not yield to anyone – in the search for truth'. Renaudot was important to journalism in the four centuries after him because he thought journalism was at the service of the truth; and though constrained by his loyalty to the king and the patronage of Richelieu, he pursued it as he could and as he understood it. The possibility of finding the truth through journalism was put into our profession from its very beginnings.

Renaudot constructed what is among the first rationales for accurate information – making the case for both its utilitarian *and* its civic value. In the Preface to the annual collection of his *Gazettes* which he wrote in 1631, he said:

> Above all, the *Gazettes* will be kept for the usefulness they have for the public and the private individual. The public, because they [the *Gazettes*] will prevent many false rumours which serve as matches to fire up internal movements and seditions . . . and private in-dividuals, each one arranging his projects according to the model of the times. Thus the merchant no longer travels to sell his wares in a town under siege, or ruined; and a soldier does not look for hire in a country where there is no war.

The next year, in a *relation* of September 1632, he asks his readers to become reporters, sending in pieces of information and con-firming (or denying) information already published: 'all are invited because of the interest they have in procuring the public good; the curious, for their own satisfaction; people of conscience, because of their zeal and their goodness in showing the right way, which is that of the truth for those who have been led astray, and to prevent the course of a lie'. Nearly four centuries later, the Internet returns readers to Renaudot's time: readers *are* becoming reporters – and columnists, and gossip writers and editors. And may thereby procure the 'public good'.

For Renaudot, the king had to be the ultimate arbiter of truth, but he lived in a time when the interests of Louis XIII/Richelieu and those of accurate information, as far as it could be ascertained, could often roughly coincide. But as journalism developed, and when practised by those in opposition to or even rebellion against their rulers, it quickly ran up against the refusal of these rulers to stop information from leaving their, or the Church's, monopoly of it. Radical journalism – the journalism which wasn't allowed, or only sporadically allowed – grew up at the same time as official, or officially sanctioned journalism. A century and a half after Renaudot's reflections on the truth, journalism was claimed as the voice, and the liberator, of the people by the revolutionary journalists of Paris. Gilles Feyel notes that 'during the Revolution, journalists exercised a magistracy of truth . . . this power of truth [was] a real counter-power to the power of the state, seen as always abusing its power, or as lying to the citizens'.

Radical journalism claimed a truth, which was always that which 'they' didn't want people to read, because the truth was dangerous, interesting and popular. In his 'Man of Taste', the eighteenth-century English poet James Branston writes that:

> Can statutes keep the British press in awe
> When that sells best, that's most against the law?

In Germany and Russia, news journalism was suppressed because of its subversive power; instead, cultural, literary and scientific journalism was permitted. This meant that these journals were made to carry 'subversive' thoughts which could not be otherwise expressed – a tradition which survived deep into the twentieth century in the Soviet Union. In the US, press freedom became linked to freedom from the colonial autocracy, Britain. Tom Paine's journalism voiced the same demand for liberty which was sweeping Europe at the time: a common anti-autocratic movement. On the banners with Liberty, was Truth.

This was a press which stood with the people against the autocracy, the peasants against the landlords, the oppressed against the imperialists, the workers against the capitalists. This version of the Truth – which at its best and most courageous, was opposition to oppression in the name, at least, of human rights – carried on an increasingly separate existence and does so still. The *Daily News* of Zimbabwe is in this mould; founded in 1999 by Wilf Mbanga, a friend and the biographer of Robert Mugabe, it struggles to survive and to bear witness to the decline of Zimbabwe into a tyranny. Mbanga wrote that once the paper began criticizing the Mugabe regime, 'my friends in the government stopped calling; some were openly hostile. Then I was arrested. I had officially become the enemy.' Totalitarian regimes – Zimbabwe is not quite there, but the end of the journey seems inevitable – must make enemies of a free media: once independent voices are choked off, the smallest publication can be a rallying point for an opposition whose force dictators cannot know, but must always fear. Journalists who try to retain some freedom have, as Vaclav Havel characterized it, only the power of the powerless. In today's global village, that powerless power can find support in the protests and voices of those in the democratic states, and must still be reckoned with by those dictators whose usually shaky finances and security force them to have some regard to international opinion (though, in too many cases, that's not much).

147

Where – as in the US and (more slowly) Britain – the press was bit by bit brought in to play an established part in political life, it soon became a power. Already, by the early nineteenth century, the first papers were breaking from the political factions in which they had been imprisoned and constrained. By 1823, William Hazlitt could write of *The Times* (founded 1788) that it was 'the greatest engine of temporary opinion in the world'. By the latter half of the century, much of the press in many countries of Europe, and in North America, was relatively free. In country after country, papers were founded to express political and other viewpoints; theirs was a great democratic flowering, a clash of views and news which greatly furthered the expansion and establishment of democratic societies. But with establishment there also came power. The press had its own interests to pursue.

Anthony Trollope's novel *The Warden* is one of the early (1854) realizations of this: a vivid bringing to life of the dilemmas, strategies and hypocrisies of journalism. Tom Towers, a writer for the *Jupiter*, exposes with the help of an old university friend the 'scandal' of an elderly curate who lives on the generous stipend paid to him from the rent of rich farmland, as the holder of the sinecure as warden to almshouses occupied by aged men of his parish. The curate is unwordly and has in any case passed some of his stipend over to the poor old men who live in the almshouses. But Towers has been given the details of the story on a plate by his friend (on the latter's momentarily irritated, and later intensely regretted, impulse) and finds the seam of outrage too easily acquired and too rich in its exploitation to be deterred from mining it.

In his sarcastic portrait of Towers, Trollope writes of one

who loved to sit silent in the corner of his club and listen to the loud chattering of politicians, and to think how they were all in his power

148

– how he could smite the loudest of them, were it worth his while to raise his pen for such a purpose. He loved to watch the great men of whom he daily wrote and flatter himself that he was greater than any of them. Each of them was responsible to his country, each of them must answer if inquired into, each of them must endure abuse with good humour, and insolence without anger. But to whom was he, Tom Towers, responsible?

It's an astonishingly good portrait of what the press – the media – would fully become a century later.

By the latter part of the nineteenth century, the partly free press had settled into being a power which both used, and was used by, other powers; which both rewarded and consumed minor talent; which could at times rise to idealism but often settled for hypocrisy. It is the world of would-be novelists and literary lions shown in George Gissing's *New Grub Street* (1891). It had also developed a routine, a method of finding out the news the press wanted. In Guy de Maupassant's *Bel Ami* (1885), the anti-hero, Georges Duroy – an ambitious and unscrupulous provincial – is described learning his trade on *La Vie Française*:

he was in continual contact with ministers and concierges, generals and policemen, princes and ponces, high class tarts and ambassadors, bishops and bawds, flashy imposters and men about town, Greeks and cabbies, waiters and all the rest, since for his own selfish purposes he became the impartial friend of all these people, taking all of them in his stride, measuring them by the same standards and sizing them up with a dispassionate eye, since he saw them all the time, all day and every day . . . he compared himself to a man who was drinking samples of so many different sorts of wine that he soon becomes unable to distinguish Château Margaux from red biddy. In a short while he had become quite an outstanding reporter . . .

149

The achievement of the 'dispassionate eye' by Duroy was general by the early decades of the twentieth century. Reporters became professionals: freeing themselves from party/faction affiliation, increasingly willing and empowered to interpret the events they reported – even the highest, such as the speeches of presidents and prime ministers. Duroy had become dispassionate; he had not become powerful – reporting was not, when he was practising it, a possible way to power. Though Duroy goes and ferrets out titbits for *La Vie Française*, they are not usually written up as stories by him; they are grist to a milling process whose miller is the editor – Walter, the anti-semitic portrait of a Jewish owner-editor whose paper is at the service of his political and financial ambitions. Duroy scavenges for mere facts or rumours to bring back to Walter and his senior associates; he chafes at his 'lowly position' and longs for the day when he can write 'authoritative political articles' – that is, articles which generally serve Walter's purpose, not in being authoritative but in putting pressure on this or that politician. The editor was not only the boss: he was the voice of the paper, in a way which ceased to be possible by the end of the nineteenth century, at least in the city papers.

By the 1920s, American reporters had found the reporters' route to power (they have remained the most powerful, relative to their politicians, with the exception of the British). The politicians had begun to see them as less an annoyance and more of a medium through which they could speak to their constituents, colleagues, opponents and the country; and the journalists began to exploit the possibilities of being such a medium. The interview – now seen as something 'natural' in journalism – passed from being an affront to the dignity of a public figure, to being the instrument of power and influence contested between public figure and journalist, which it has remained. Technology came to their aid: stenography, the typewriter, the telegraph all meant that reporters could work faster

150

and produce more. The editors themselves became professionals; the Walter figure bifurcated into owners (who could indeed, like James Gordon Bennett, Joseph Pulitzer or William Randolph Hearst, be de facto editors-in-chief, ferociously interventionist) and editors, who were hired and fired, often very rapidly. The sheer popularity of newspapers, their greater size as advertising in them grew in synchronization with the vast expansion of the consumer sector which newspapers did so much to make possible, meant that the editor was pushed further into the background – even if he retained a good deal of power over his reporters.

The early editor dealt directly with the politician: he got the important documents and, in the case of speeches, simply put them verbatim in the paper, without the intervention of a reporter interpreting the speech by setting it into a context. One can see a 200-year development in reportorial power in flashes, through the reporting of the US president's address to Congress. In the last week of October 1791, the *Boston Gazette* reported President George Washington's speech to Congress by announcing that, on Monday 24 October, a joint committee of Congress waited on the president, who agreed to address them the following day. In a report dated 25 October, one sentence announced Washington's arrival in the Congress; the paper then gives his speech verbatim, starting at the beginning and ending at the end – a practise followed by Soviet papers until the collapse of Communism. By the end of the nineteenth century, some scene setting and judicious abridgement of the key parts of the speech are permitted. By the first years of the twentieth century, reporters have begun to comment on the important parts of it; the *New York Times* wrote of William Howard Taft's speech in 1910 that he 'announced the practical abandonment of the great legislative programme with which he began his administration'. Thereafter, the comment becomes progressively freer – until it begins to shoulder the mere speeches out of the way.

Wind forward to Watergate in 1972, and we see an editor – Ben Bradlee – torn between his excitement that his reporters, Carl Bernstein and Bob Woodward, are on to something and his frustration with his inability to do the reporting himself. 'I hate trusting anybody,' the Bradlee figure, played by Jason Robards, is made to say in the film, *All the President's Men*, which immortalizes (and exaggerates) the *Washington Post's* part in Richard Nixon's downfall, showing the editor/owner cede the foreground to the reporter. The latter is the centre of the action: the moral fulcrum of the public arena. On the reporter's shoulders rests the honesty of the public sphere.

Come to the present: the reproduction, for the Hutton Inquiry, of the e-mail correspondence within the BBC after the Gilligan broadcast reveals the extraordinary passivity of the BBC editors – from those directly in charge of the 'Today' programme to the editor-in-chief of the BBC – in the face of a report whose veracity they would not challenge, or even examine. A reporter had reported it and it had been questioned by Alastair Campbell in Downing Street. It must thus be blindly endorsed – even up to the board of governors – and the objections be regarded as unworthy of consideration. From editorial omnipotence to editorial weakness is not a route every media organization has travelled, but it is a common one, as our times privilege display, controversy, personality and celebrity; and the editor, once the sole voice of the paper, is reduced to one who voices complaints *sotto voce* after the event.

The reporter's climb to the mastery of the airwaves, which we saw in the few minutes of conversation between correspondent and presenter on 29 May 2003, was steady. By degrees through the twentieth century, the reporter intervened to give to an expanding audience the tools to interpret the speeches and the proposals and the legislation. Bit by bit, the reporters became less partisan, and strove for a neutrality, an objectivity. They began to see themselves

152

as experts, professionals. They were no longer, like Bel Ami, the scavengers for an editor who, with a few other editorial writers, composed a paper which was run in his own, or a faction's, interest. They began to see the world for themselves, and to describe it – albeit largely in formulaic ways – independently.

Sometimes, very independently: one of the early and remaining glories of the journalistic profession was a rare (until the last few decades) woman journalist, Ida Tarbell. In an extraordinary 24 instalments across two years (1904–6) in the monthly magazine *McLure's*, Tarbell wrote an exposé of the Standard Oil Company of America, then a ravening monster which sought monopoly control of America's oil fields. When she did this investigation, she was a middle-aged woman (mid-forties) in a man's world, who had been *McLure's* literary editor, exposing the inner workings of a company that had shown itself to be ruthless. One of the historians of the oil business says of her that 'she would not be stayed. An indefatigable and exhaustive researcher, she also became a sleuth, absorbed and obsessed by her case, convinced that she was on to a great story.' Her exposés, later written up as a book – *The History of Standard Oil* (1904) – played to a powerful mood of the time: progressivism, an amalgam of political reform, agitation for social justice, protection of the consumer and the 'little guy' and greater transparency in public affairs – the last of these the great cause of, and rationale for, more vigorous and independent journalism.

Tarbell's series was hugely significant in relation to the way in which journalism approached the world and became part of it. The magazine itself was owned and edited by a talented entrepreneur, Samuel McClure, who wanted to use it to expose what was happening in the country, especially in its economic development. In doing so, he helped to establish what has remained the summit of US journalism: the current affairs journal, with the resources, ambition and writing talent to describe at length both the detail and the scope of social, political and economic change. And Tarbell's series was of an importantly different order from the great journalistic moments that preceded it – such as William Howard Russell's despatches from Crimea for *The Times*, or Emile Zola's campaign against Dreyfus' imprisonment in *Le Figaro*, *L'Aurore* and elsewhere. The first was reportage which had broken the code of 'honourable' deceit which surrounded the doings of army officers and which caused the resignation of the government of the day and, in Anthony Smith's words, was a decisive spur to the role newspapers were assuming in the late nineteenth century, that of 'brokerage between authority and the middle class in Victorian society'. The second was a declamation of the truth as a sword which would – literally in Dreyfus' case – set one free: the fury of an already famous writer who could use his intellect, freedom and conscience in a great cause, and who saw in journalism the possibility of having 'attention focused on reality, a search for truth, inquiry, the publication of texts, which allows things to be shown as they are'.

Tarbell's way of 'showing things as they are' was different and went further. She shared the keenness of vision and iconoclasm of Russell and the indignation of Zola, but she put both on a more long-term, structured footing than either a brilliant piece of coverage of an extraordinary event, or a spurt of generous indignation over a despicable act. She assembled a mass of documentary evidence from a variety of sources over a long period of time, using her own and others' research, interviews, eye witnesses, documents and reports of the experience of (many) others. Where Russell exposed a situation and Zola blasted a crime, she gave a narrative. All three had, consciously or not, worked to increase the effective bounds of citizenship. Russell did it by showing what was done in the citizens' (and taxpayers') name by those directing the army in war – the most notable, and most expensive, of state projects. Zola did it by exposing the perversion of justice, in a state whose citizens should have been – but were not – ruled equally by laws. Tarbell did it by publishing an immense amount of information about a company which was refashioning the US economy. She rejected the title of 'muckraker', current (and popular) at the time to describe the politically driven exposés of business and government, arguing, 'I was convinced that the public they [the muckrakers] were trying to stir would weary of vituperation, that if you were to secure permanent results, the mind must be convinced' – a great text for journalism.

Russell, Zola and Tarbell were informed by a desire to use their talent to right wrongs; all were on the 'liberal' side of their times and countries, and were resented, even hated, by conservatives. They set a pattern of exposure, denunciation and documented revelation which showed the power of journalism – and showed journalists their power.

Most journalism, of course, was not like that and has not been since – though many have sought to be Russell without his courage, Zola without his cause, Tarbell without her labour. Most journalism became and remained a profession, of sorts; certainly it became professionalized and more dignified. By-lines crept slowly into US papers in the second decade of the twentieth century, at first only for the star reporters, then more generally. The great political occasions of the day – conventions, debates, speeches – were reported as events and subject to 'expert' analysis and comment. While a newspaper would condemn a politician belonging to a camp other than its own, it would increasingly employ writers who could summarize the event and give an analysis which did not depend on ideological bias. Journalism, especially American journalism, strove for an objectivity which was if not above, certainly beside, party, seeking writers who could strike a note which mixed rapid reporting with the judgement of experience. Newspapers came to value the reputation of independence – independence of judgement and independence from faction. Many papers have underlined the point by calling themselves 'independent'.

Ideological affiliation was not, however, left behind. Instead, the two principles – of attachment to a political position, and of independence from one – both continued to exist in different papers, or even in different media cultures, and do so still. Anthony Smith writes that:

> throughout the [twentieth] century, the main intellectual tension among newspapers has been between the ethic which demands 'independence' and an older ethic, surviving in many places, by which the newspaper is supposed to belong to one of several competing ideologies. A steady gulf has grown between American and European practises, the former dedicated to a journalism of neutral, factual information untainted by party, unblemished by influence; the latter still clinging, half contradictorily, to the view that journalists should carry their party affiliations open to view.

That – written some 25 years ago – is no longer as true as it was, but it's still a useful way to look at the world. In fact, it might be a useful direction for journalism to take again. At least it might make things clearer – if we knew, upfront, with what agenda the journalist was approaching the world. But it would only be really useful if the journalist was prepared to stick with that agenda him- or herself. One reason why journalism is unpopular, especially with publicly accountable people like politicians, scientists, medical workers and public officials, is that the reporters and the commentators keep popping up to slam them to both the right and the left of them – and they're the same people. Many public figures thus conclude that journalists don't believe in anything but slamming people. Many journalists believe that they should slam everyone equally. And that that is balance, or even independence, or even the truth.

The lessons which earlier ways of doing journalism taught – especially that of Ida Tarbell – are often lost, or misremembered. Tarbell's investigation was both an explanation of corporate behaviour and a chronicle of social change. She gave substance to the explicit and implicit criticisms she made of Standard Oil by the work she did in detailing what the company did, and how. She showed what investigation is capable of: at its best, of non-polemical enlightenment. That has been the promise of all journalism at times; it is specifically the promise of public service broadcasting – indeed, I would argue, its only call on the taxpayer's pocket. Is journalism able to keep that promise any more? And especially – is public broadcasting worth supporting any more?

Controversy uncovers truth was the claim in John Stuart Mill's *Essay on Liberty*, one of free journalism's basic texts. Mill argues that 'complete liberty of contradicting and disproving our opinion is the very condition which justifies us in assuming truth for purposes of action; and on no other terms can a being with human faculties have any rational assurance of being right'. The idea stands behind a movement away from any attempt at objectivity; towards a broadcasting culture which accepts that objectivity is impossible, and that thus bias should be openly expressed in news and current affairs coverage. Reflecting on the coverage of the Iraq war, Fletcher Crossman, a US teacher of English who had worked as a broadcast journalist in the UK, said of the difference between the two major Anglo-Saxon media cultures that 'the political bias of its [US] news stations is open, brash and strangely addictive. The British bias is subtle, covert and shielded by the myth of objectivity.'

157

Calling for the BBC to drop what he also sees as its 'myth of objectivity' – a myth, he says, because most of the presenters and reporters are *Guardian*-reading liberals – the conservative commentator Peter Hitchens argues that the BBC 'should match every one of [the liberal presenters] with an avowed conservative, so that no politician or man of power is ever again interviewed by a sympathizer, and current affairs programmes crackle with open and legitimate controversy, *the kind that uncovers the truth*' (my italics).

That may be the Mill conception of how truth emerges, but in practise it doesn't, as any contemporary discussion programme shows. In his book *Breaking the News* James Fallows reproduces a March 1995 discussion from NBC's 'Meet the Press', in which President Clinton's main economic adviser, Laura Tyson, discussed the federal deficit with John Kasich, a Republican Congressman, Democratic Senator Bill Bradley, and *Washington Post* columnist David Broder – the discussion moderated by the presenter, Tim Russert. The explicit aim of the programme is to illuminate the truth of the given theme through the clash of opinions. Here is the end of the discussion (it wasn't much better at the beginning):

Tyson: Look, the point is the deficit – we're not talking here – you are not talking about what . . .

Russert: Your budget plan – excuse me.

Kasich: You need a referee.

Russert: I'm being a fact checker, I'm being a fact checker. The budget you put forward . . .

Tyson: You are.

Russert: . . . puts together $200bn deficits. David, you jump in here about . . .

Tyson: We agree. We agree with that.

Russert: Please David.

Tyson: I agree with that.

Broder: Yeah.

Tyson: I did not say that was not true, did I?

Russert: Robert Reich [Labour Secretary in Clinton's first term] on this programme said . . .

Tyson: I did not say that was not true.

Russert: 'A balanced budget is not his goal.'

Tyson: Look, what I said is, we have – are bringing down – look, if you have a company . . .

Kasich: Your deficit's going up by $30bn of your budget, Doctor.

Fallows comments on this, and other, passages by saying that 'the discussion shows that are supposed to add to public understanding may actually reduce it, by hammering home the message that "issues" don't matter except as items for politicians to squabble about.' On television, and to a lesser degree on radio, programmes in which politicians, or public figures, or commentators are confronted with hostile questioning do not elicit truth, but defensiveness, or ritual jousting. The stakes are too high to allow one's guard down: an admission, even a minor one, will be treated as a scandal; a deviation, even a minor one, from party or government policy seen as the harbinger of a split. Leading politicians – including two cabinet ministers to whom I spoke about the media on terms of anonymity – both regarded as naïve the proposal that they led in discussing issues openly, in the way they do privately; that is, with sometimes strong disagreement, but also with the underlying assumption that agreement and compromise must be the result. Both said that they would destroy their government by such a stance – because the media would fasten on difference and seek to amplify it to faction and then to split – and on a central issue, this could paralyse, or actually split, the administration.

Even where the programme is more carefully structured than the example above – where, for example, one questioner of opposing view to the interviewee (or at least, in Hitchens' formula, not 'a sympathizer') puts questions and allows time for the answer – the polemical-antagonistic nature of the questions is bound to elicit a zero-sum game encounter. That is, the interviewee could assume that any slip, error or admission would be built on for aggressive effect. Indeed, it was with just this in mind that politicians have built up apparatuses of defence and control around their public appearances.

We have a foretaste of what the modern world would make of the modernized Mill position – one to which we can expect many more people to be drawn, if and as we don't succeed in retaining, and modernizing, what an 'objective' public service broadcaster would do. The foretaste is US talk radio – liberated from any duty to be fair or balanced by the Federal Communications Commission of the Reagan era and by a judgement in the US Court of Appeals which overturned the 1949 Fairness Doctrine. Talk radio is dominated very largely – as Rupert Murdoch gladly confessed – by conservatives; but liberals, unfortunately, are planning to get in on the act too.

Unfortunately, because the evidence seems to be that liberals will emulate the conservatives in the way in which they broadcast; and the experience of the conservative talk shows so far is that they play on resentment, myth and insult at the expense of anything resembling the truth. Though some truths may be uncovered in the flow of verbiage and bare-knuckled argument with liberals, including liberal callers – both discrete facts which should be uncovered, and larger truths about society, or the media itself – the overwhelming impression left is of bile, prejudice and a view of the world composed of mistruths, about the enemies whom talk show radio hosts see all around. Talk radio requires named or generic enemies to succeed. Where Limbaugh lit on the

160

Clinton administration in all its works, the first liberal break-through in talk radio also found that identifying and hammering an enemy was the way to success. The black Washington station, WOL, took off in 1986 when it targeted the *Washington Post*, which had run a magazine story on a black rapper charged with murder, together with a column sympathizing with shopkeepers who barred their doors against young blacks. The resentment unleashed against the *Post* – which caused it to apologize on WOL in the persons of its editor and publisher – made its ratings soar, saved it from bankruptcy and allowed its founder and chief presenter, Cathy Hughes, to build up a $3 billion-worth network of stations known as Radio One.

All talk show hosts use abuse, exaggeration, accusations and character assassination to build their audiences – precisely the characteristics which politicians must eschew if they are to run, or be a responsible opposition in an advanced, pluralist state. They rely on an audience which supports the resentment they claim they feel – a resentment nearly always aimed at the government, or liberal/conservative authority figures. When Hillary Clinton spoke, as the Monica Lewinsky affair broke around the White House, of a 'right-wing conspiracy' aimed against her husband's presidency, she was only partly right. Though there were some elements of conspiracy among those politicians, activists and journalists who pursued Clinton, the more important matter was that, what drove the attack was not conspiracy, but a mood. It is an attitude which is pursued not for party advantage – for it can turn against party quickly, as the Republicans found in the mid-1990s, when their pragmatic compromises of the kind any democratic party must make were treated as treachery by the talk show hosts, led by Rush Limbaugh, which had lauded them before.

Limbaugh's career as a bad mouther – 'did you know there's a White House dog?' he asked once, during a TV appearance, while

161

holding up a picture of Chelsea Clinton, then 13 – made him very powerful, and tremendously admired, on the right. Tony Blankley, the former press secretary for Newt Gingrich, who led the Republican surge in the early–mid-1990s, wrote that 'After Newt, Rush was the single most important person in securing a Republican majority on the House of Representatives after years of Democratic party rule. Rush's powerful voice was the indispensable factor . . . at a time when almost the entire media establishment ignored or distorted our message of renewal, Rush carried (and often improved) the message to the heartland.' Limbaugh is the political pits; but liberals want to follow him down there because – as Blankley testifies – he makes winners.

Eric Alterman wrote of right-wing radio that it had showed a 'deceitful dynamic of ideological extremism against which truth – and liberalism – have little chance to compete'. He wrote before US liberals began, in an organized way, to try to do just that, but he remains right. Neither truth nor liberalism can compete with defamation and smear, and liberals trying to do so will lose both.

And they are trying. Jason Zengerle, who reported on the success of right talk and the emulation of left talk, wrote that in November 2003, a group of senior Democratic senators, among them Hillary Clinton and Tom Daschle, gathered in the Capitol Hill home of one of their number to raise money for Democracy Radio, a would-be liberal shock-jock station. In a speech to the gathering, Democratic Senator Bob Graham of Florida told his fellow guests that where the left-wing shock-jock Randi Rhodes broadcast – on the radio station WJNO in Florida's West Palm Beach – no Republican could win, a strikingly similar endorsement to that given to Limbaugh by Newt Gingrich's press secretary. Rhodes' four-hour afternoon broadcasts have included accusations that Osama Bin Laden plotted the 9/11 attack on the Twin Towers because he was disgusted with the close relations between the Bush family (senior and junior) and the corruption of the Saudi royals; the attacks were thus aimed not against America, but against Bush personally. Rhodes has also claimed that Saddam Hussein had been taken many months before his advertised date of capture, and kept secretly in order to be revealed in December 'as a Christmas present from the president'. When Zengerle asked Rhodes why leading Democrats were prepared to laud her, and to raise money for stations which would put her on the air, she said that she had told the senators: 'our purpose as talk-show hosts is to say things you can't say'. The answer reveals a state of mind which assumes that the public world is a sham, full of events which have been manipulated for the public; one where the enemy, however repre-sented, is capable of limitless deception, limitless evil. This has the same paranoid basis as right-wing talk radio.

The writer Fareed Zakaria remarked that liberal journalists are often journalists first and liberals second, but that conservative journalists are conservatives first and journalists second. This is true only of some, and usually American, conservative journalists, but it is more generally true of journalism, in this sense. Modern journalism was to an important degree constructed by liberals; the early, and later, triumphs of disclosure, protest and investigation have been done, generally, under a liberal impetus – either personal or as part of a movement such as progressivism.

Insofar as conservatives stand for religion, family and social hierarchy, they will find most journalists to be culturally sceptical; because their 'bias' will be against that which is beyond rational explanation because of faith, and against that which justifies itself by reference to tradition and patriarchal (or other) time-honoured authority. Even journalism of the right tends to obey these rules – that is, its reasoning is secular and pragmatic. It doesn't rest on either divine revelation or an ordering of the world which 'has always been like that'. Indeed, the newest form of US-inspired conservatism – neo-conservatism – is radically opposed to both faith and tradition. Both the politicians and the writers within that tradition must grapple with the contradictions inherent in their approach; that is, that they are anti-tradition radicals abroad who rely for at least some of their domestic electoral base on traditional, religious, hierarchy-observing conservatives.

Journalism run on liberal lines which privileges reason, proof, argument and accountability can't marry with the kind of ersatz, no-holds-barred 'angry person' journalism of shock-jock radio and its imitators. If liberals succeed in starting talk radio of that kind, they will be collaborating in what they accuse conservatives of doing – degrading democratic practise. In any case, truth can't, in practise, be reached that way. Indeed, the state of mind which reflects on what might be true in public affairs is probably discouraged rather than encouraged by this twenty-first-century son of Mill, because it is led to dwell on grievances and to amplify them in the public arena. Talk radio has engineered a fantastic reversal of rightists' consistent stance over the centuries, leading them to abandon the principle that a society is best composed of sturdy individuals who stand on their own feet and work out their destiny themselves. Right-wing talk radio screamed: 'It's their fault! The inequities, and hassles, and unhappinesses of your life are because of these liberals! Blame them!' Now, liberals are seeking to even the game – by doing the same thing. The losers will be a public which seeks to orient itself in a complex world. Talk radio says, implicitly: don't even try to know what's what by reason. Stick with the prejudices you know. Blame them!

Shock-jock radio's one merit is that it's openly what it is. We know that it creates an atmosphere because it's popular: people respond to it. It has been widely believed that Limbaugh touched off popular beliefs, fears and protests which had not been previously articulated by liberal media and that is probably true.

However, where left-wing shock-jock radio has succeeded, it has done so with the same tools – of personal character assassination, unsubstantiated (and often unsubstantiatable) allegations and appeals to prejudice or resentment – as those deployed by the right-wing equivalents. The point may be less the underlying ideological, or social, or religious, beliefs – as the mobilization of anger and bile, always present in most of us, but often lacking focus and the dignity of being dressed up in political finery.

Great truths trump little mistakes. In the wake of the Kelly affair, most journalists thought Andrew Gilligan had got something wrong. But very many believed he had got more right. In what should become known as the Gilligan defence, lots of journalists – and others who weren't journalists – wrote or gave interviews, saying that the most important thing about Gilligan's report was that it focused attention on something fishy going on in the government-secret service world. They believed that we citizens obviously had been 'spun' very heavily by, among other things, the dossier about which Gilligan had made his report; and that it was a real public service to get that into the public arena in some form, even if not wholly accurately. If, as an analogy, a building were about to collapse and someone shouted 'fire', you would be grateful for the warning to get out – even if the warning was itself inaccurate.

That Gilligan's report was quite comprehensively wrong is not seen as vitiating that defence. And it has been made by some of the doyens of the profession. Anthony Sampson, in his new *Anatomy*, writes (after criticizing the report and the BBC) that:

> while the BBC had exaggerated and distorted some allegations, it had played an indispensable role in revealing the truth behind the misleading dossiers which the government had used to justify the

165

war. And at a time when the parliamentary opposition was hope-lessly weak, the BBC with all its faults and unaccountability had acted as the most effective opposition during a crisis.

John Humphrys, who was personally and considerably involved in the original broadcast, wrote in his regular *Sunday Times* column that 'it is no good saying we must report only what is true because what is true cannot always be proven . . . what we should always keep in the back of our minds is that even the best journalists must sometimes be free to be wrong.'

These are serious positions: they address the inevitable nature of journalism as a profession which at critical times cannot always be sure of the premises of what it is saying. They also address the need for democratic societies to be alerted to dangers and hidden facts which governments may have little interest in clarifying and oppositions have little more such interest in – in the case of the war in Iraq, because the main opposition party agreed with the government on the need for war.

Further, where journalists are not free to be wrong they are also usually not free to be right. In much of continental Europe, laws protecting the privacy and the dignity of the individual are stronger than in the UK, and are used – as is immunity from prosecution – to shield from view much in the political and business world, from the merely embarrassing to the blatantly corrupt. The case of France is a clear one: the media, faced with a political establishment against some of whose members serious charges are made, can only go so far, and that distance is usually defined by what examining magistrates discover. A journalism which investigates and which, like Ida Tarbell's, invests swathes of time and intelligence in figuring out what is happening in one or other part of the state or the economy is not wholly absent. *Le Monde*, in particular, has under the team of chief editor Jean-Marie Colombani and editorial director Edwy Plenel taken a (much criticized) route of greater openness both to popular culture and to investigation. But the limits are tight, even stifling; the close collaboration between media and politicians is in part an insurance by the latter, conscious or not, that the media's potential for exposure is kept in check by a constant interchange of favours in the form of news and gossip (*naturellement, c'est OFF*).

British journalists largely do, and should, avoid being muzzled. But where they further claim the right to be wrong at times in the service of a higher truth than that contained in the mere facts of the story – not a position which most American journalists would take – this runs a high risk of being merely a self-serving rationale for bad journalism. Journalists *are* free to be wrong under the law, which, as Humphrys noted in the same column, is now more liberal after a judgement on the case of the *Sunday Times* v Albert Reynolds, the former prime minister of Ireland, laid down that a mistake on the part of the newspaper could be in the public interest. In the US, the right to be (by European standards) not just wrong but grossly defamatory of named individuals is strongly protected – a protection indispensable to the success of shock-jock radio. In such an environment, journalists have a legal, and claim a moral, protection against the consequences of being wrong, a position enjoyed by no other profession. Not just does no other profession have it, journalism itself would regard such an exculpation as an outrage.

The defence is, of course, the greater public good. But such a defence is open to others on similar bases. Lawyers and police officers might claim that a minor falsification of evidence which results in the conviction of a dangerous criminal would be in the public good. Doctors and nurses might claim that a quiet – known only to themselves – termination of a life of agony benefits both the patient and relatives. Politicians and civil servants might claim that a lie, or a concealment of facts at least for a time, could enable a large project in the public interest to go ahead where otherwise it would be blocked by interest groups' opposition.

Indeed, all of these groups *do* claim that, usually privately. They claim it privately because it is impossible to justify publicly: impossible, because of the self-evident dangers. Where does falsification of evidence end? How does a judgement on the termination of life avoid giving God-like powers to medical staff? How can the lie for good ends fail to set a precedent for the lie in general? Rudimentary liberal practise rules these manoeuvres out, accepting, as it must, the evident and often hideous downsides – in monsters un-arrested, in agony prolonged, in beneficial projects not undertaken. The tug between the workings of liberal democratic principles and the sacrifices they entail define much of our public argument, necessarily.

Why should journalism have a position above all this? Why should journalism not have to accept a 'liberal downside', that if it cannot prove the case it makes when it tells a story because the journalist cannot get the facts, then it must accept that the story doesn't get written, or broadcast? Would that not be a stimulus to try harder to get the facts? Is the public interest in its case so much larger than those affecting the police, lawyers, medical professionals, officials, politicians?

The answer is yes – at times. No, at (most) other times. Cases in extremis can easily be imagined: a renegade group within government bent on subverting democracy; a very large malfeasance or corruption in public authorities; a terrorist group planning to commit an outrage; a vast miscarriage of justice. In such cases, if and when they arise, getting the facts wrong and the story right is the kind of public service easily recognized after the event. Less cinematically, though, the cases tend to fall into that area well known to all who have to look at evidence and base some sort of story on it – as police officers, lawyers, doctors, nurses, civil servants and politicians all do. Clarity is hard: evidence is contradictory; people disagree, both in good faith and bad. Complex and important cases – stories – have to be built up slowly and with care, more akin to difficult jigsaw puzzles than to a flash revelation. Journalists who do stories on the latter basis will often find them wrong: little is as simple as a sudden understanding of an event; almost everything needs a context, almost everything is modified by context – the more context, the more modification. Nothing, not even journalism, relieves us of the need to make judgements.

A case made by the media commentator Michael Massing against the *New York Times'* coverage of the evidence of Iraqi weapons of mass destruction – the same highly charged arena into which Andrew Gilligan ventured – lets us see the difficulties. Massing charged the *Times*, and two of its journalists – Judith Miller and Michael Gordon – with ignoring evidence, which other journalists published, on the doubts in the intelligence and weapons inspection communities about the story that was told by the Bush administration on Iraqi WMD. Miller and Gordon were among the most experienced writers on the subject in the world: both had published well-regarded books on the subject. Miller in particular had travelled widely to interview Iraqi exiles; and both she and Gordon were in constant touch with administration and other officials – under successive administrations – who confirmed the exiles' claims that Saddam had retained WMD and was developing, or could develop, more. Massing says they largely ignored, or downplayed, the evidence that many experts didn't believe that Saddam was able to develop WMD (both journalists strongly denied this to him when he interviewed them and, as Massing admits, Gordon published a front-page account – there were others, by other writers – on the divisions among the experts on Iraqi WMD).

The reports which were published in the *Times* were mirrored by many other publications and channels all over the world. Most carried stories and comment warning against the Iraqis' possession of WMD because that is what most weapons inspectors, government experts, exiles and apparently Saddam Hussein believed. Had, for example, most newspapers in the US or in the UK published stories based only or largely on the testimony of those who *doubted* Saddam's possession of WMD, there would have been a substantial rumbling from people who did not believe it. Had the CIA or the British intelligence services advised the government that Saddam had no WMD, there would have been a very large internal revolt, which would have reached the media. Philip Bobbitt, who was director of security in the National Security Council in Clinton's administration, has observed that division among secret service officers over the meaning of partial, contested and contradictory information is a fact of life in the intelligence world. The extra factor is that the media, with less and less of a delay, pick up on the divisions and magnify them – thus giving the 'dissidents' within the services a way of publicizing views about which they feel strongly and have seen suppressed.

Is it good to know about these debates? In theory it is; we live in a world in which we honour the notion that the more disclosure, the better for both government and governed, at least in the long run and I don't see any reason to dissent from that. But it has a downside too – a big one. Revelation and disclosure are presented by the media, largely for commercial reasons, with great fanfare. The fact of the revelation – the exclusive – is regarded as at least as important as the content of the story. But usually we are given no way of knowing if the dissidence is important, well based or even broadly shared. The journalist is often little more able to evaluate the reliability of either side in the debate than the reader or viewer. A time when recourse to an authority – university professor, medical specialist, economist – was seen as largely clinching the matter is gone, in part because many experts have hired themselves out to commercial or lobby interests and devalue their expertise. The expert is no longer regarded as much more than a convenience for proving a point: if she or he doesn't do so, then she or he is discarded or devalued – as was Brian Hutton, when his report was inconveniently supportive of the government. We are usually given a story of conflict; we're usually not given a story of substance.

Many stories so based – Gilligan's was one of them – have something going for them. Debates are a way of pointing towards truth, even if they don't usually tell us what the truth is. So though it is right that what is true cannot always be proven, it is also the case that what is revealed is not always – is rarely – 'true', in any sense that has real meaning for us. The revelation is, at best, only a beginning: the rest of the thread has to be pulled out.

Should we forget about objectivity? One of the greatest tests for a journalist to remain neutral is reporting conflict – both because of the difficulties and dangers and because of the temptation to take sides. It's thus a good test, at an extreme, of the robustness of the objective approach. And war reporting is, indeed, one of the most debated kinds of journalism, which has produced many memoirs from foreign correspondents, who often shuttle from conflict to conflict – itself a comment on the fascination of broadcasters for wars, and their relative boredom with other international issues which may be as significant. The long-time BBC correspondents Kate Adie, Martin Bell (now retired) and John Simpson have all written memoirs. These are mainly stories of derring-do, for all three – and many others working for broadcasters and newspapers – were obliged to draw deeply on reserves of courage in order to continue, day after day and year after year, to face considerable danger.

171

Of these war reporters, only Martin Bell has produced an important reflection on the nature of journalism – one which raises the issue which has tormented broadcasters, and especially the BBC, for decades: that of objectivity. He does so by drawing the lesson from one of the more important of our contemporary ethical crucibles – the siege of the Bosnian capital of Sarajevo, which happened over a two-year period in the early 1990s. It was a time when, Bell believes, journalism became a 'moral profession'.

It was certainly a time when journalism, in its search for greater power, won a decisive battle against its great rival, politics. Neither profession has fully recovered its equilibrium: politicians who think about these matters still feel guilt and journalists still feel smug. The battle between them for the moral high ground, one of the most prominent cultural themes of these times, continues, presently cast in the slippery form of a struggle for the possession of the 'truth' in the matter of the reasons for the US and Britain going to war with Iraq.

Martin Bell was BBC television's main man in Sarajevo in this 'crucible' period, and is a very important person in these moral wars. A man who had the stamina and physical courage to be a successful television war correspondent in his fifties, he became an independent member of parliament in 1997 when he won, with Labour support, the solidly Conservative seat of Tatton. Its sitting MP, Neil Hamilton, had become perhaps the most unpopular MP of his generation. Like the contrast that his once ubiquitous white suit presented to the dull panorama of middle-aged British men's fashion, Bell has highlighted himself against backgrounds which he has represented as brutal, corrupt, mendacious, or conformist.

In the 1990s, Bell wrote two books – *In Harm's Way* and *Accidental MP* – and published a third in 2003, *Through Gates of Fire*. In this, he draws deeply on the moral capital he acquired as a war reporter, as an independent MP and as an anti-celebrity

172

celebrity. In the second of these roles, he presents himself as a severe critic of the constraints of party, political ambition and lack of moral fibre in the political and media classes. In the first, he proposes a 'journalism of attachment' – an 'engaged' journalism, which bears witness to horrors and stirs the conscience both of the mass audience and of public men and women who have the power and command the resources to put a stop to horrors.

Bell is a star, and talks like one. That is, he assumes – reasonably in view of past experience – that interviewers want him to talk about himself. Thus when I asked him, in an interview he gave me to promote his book published in 2003, if he thought television news and current affairs had dumbed down, he said, 'I see it happening. The smartest decision I made last year was not to appear on "Celebrity Big Brother",' an apparent non sequitur, until you work out that he means the story to indicate that television seeks to reduce serious journalists like him to the level of vacuity. Then he began a complaint that war reporting was now done from hotel roofs – a phenomenon he first noticed, he said, when reporting from El Salvador in the early 1980s, 'and I was the only poor sod in the trenches'. The alternative to hotel roofs was 'smartly dressed blokes in front of video walls' – a sign that television executives 'want more control over the awkward squad, people like me'.

He thinks that independent television has stopped doing serious news and that the BBC has become consumed with celebrity; that reporting has become more about performance than the imparting of information; and that the pressures of 24-hour news mean that 'too many people don't know what's happening on the ground'. But like any celebrity, he knows that he is the story, he sells the books and he is the reason producers want him on television shows. So much of what you hear is self-serving; for a man who had presented himself as the epitome of stubborn, independent-minded Englishness, he is quite un-English in his self-promotion. You must remind yourself, as Bell tells you in many different ways that he showed great courage and is very principled, that he *did* show great courage and that he *does* have strong principles.

His main principle – the journalism of attachment – is increasingly popular in the media. Indeed, during the Iraq war, those newspapers, especially the *Daily Mirror* and the *Independent*, which took an anti-war position, were fiercely 'attached' to it, in their reporting as well as in their editorials and columns – more so than those newspapers which supported the war. But newspapers are usually 'attached', and should be. The radical step taken by Martin Bell, however, is to advocate a journalism of attachment for the BBC – the public broadcaster. Implicitly, Bell is asking the BBC to respect the political choices and biases of reporters who claim a moral right to make these choices and to have these biases. The 'journalism of attachment' is thus a radical step: it's important to recognize that, and to understand what it entails, in practise and in principle.

Bell defined it to me first by a negative. 'It's not polemical. John Pilger [the journalist and broadcaster who believes US imperialism is the greatest danger in the contemporary world] is too polemical for me. What I mean is a journalism which *cares* as well as *knows*.' Bell *knew* that war in Bosnia was giving rise to massacres, rape, looting and misery; he *cared* enough to go beyond the reportage and to call for intervention by those states – above all Britain, his main customer – with the capacity to stop it. An incoming mortar, he writes, knocked 'detachment' out of him – although why it should have had that effect, he doesn't say. I put to him the case of a journalist who believed that membership of the EU is destructive of British values. If such a journalist believes he knows this, and has proof of it, and cares about his fellow countrymen, shouldn't he

174

bear witness to his knowledge and concern, and call for an end to Britain's EU membership? 'That's the job of a columnist,' said Bell. But hadn't he done just such a columnist's job when, in April 1996, he made a plea for intervention in his last news broadcast from Sarajevo (the passage is reproduced with pride in *Through Gates of Fire*)? Bell said in the broadcast, a powerful and sombre one, that:

> There are surely some lessons to be learned here if this ordeal is not to be repeated – important lessons, diplomatic and military. Diplomatic: that action not taken can be just as dangerous as any action being considered; that procrastination, delay, the expedient diplomatic fudge – all these can cost lives. They can and in Bosnia they have. And the military lesson is surely that, if there's no agreement between the parties, then a measure of enforcement is going to be necessary. And if you're going to threaten force you have to be willing to use force, and to bear the costs and casualties that go with it.

Wasn't this an opinion? I asked him. More, it was an opinion calling for a direct political and military decision; for soldiers to risk their lives and to kill others, who would almost certainly include the innocent. Bell, a little curtly, repeated what he has said in his book: 'it was a decision arising out of three and a half years of experience.' These three and a half years were spent when the governments of Europe and North America, particularly Britain's, were committed to not intervening. The prevailing line was that the Balkans was a place of ancient enmities, best kept out of. The British foreign secretary of the day, Douglas Hurd, made a speech in which he spoke slightingly of people like Bell as the 'something must be done brigade'.

If not a brigade, the shifting collection of men and women who covered the Bosnian horrors were certainly a platoon whose esprit

175

de corps, the product of shared dangers and pressures, issued forth in a bitter indictment of politicians' spinelessness. Alan Little, presently (2004) BBC bureau chief in Paris and another correspondent who came and went continually to Bosnia during this time, told me that one night, in the Holiday Inn where the journalists stayed, a group got out the whisky bottle and a copy of A. J. P. Taylor's *Causes of the Second World War*. 'We took turns in reading out paragraphs which you could directly transpose from then to now. We read Hurd back into Halifax [the pre-war, proappeasement foreign secretary].'

But Little – who did not become famous as a result of the war, despite writing, with Laura Silber, the *Financial Times* correspondent in Belgrade at the time, a fine book, *The Death of Yugoslavia* – does not share Bell's view of a journalism of attachment.

> I share Martin's view that there should have been an intervention. I agreed that the line 'everyone is guilty and so nothing can be done', was terrible. But Martin thought that war was awful and must be stopped through advocacy. I thought reporting should show that the Serbs' drive to extend their area was the motive force behind the war, and that once that was shown, the conclusion would speak for itself. You couldn't be an advocate and work for the BBC. The *Guardian* or the *Independent* could do it, fine, but not the BBC.

Little's view – it was shared by such reporters as John Burns of the *New York Times*, who has accused many of his fellow reporters in Iraq of not reporting the scale of Saddam's atrocities – was sharply at odds with Bell's. The latter believed that war was a horror, like earthquake and famine, that it had to be stopped and that the duty of an informed reporter was to testify as to what must be done to stop it; Bell wished to turn the 'something must be done brigade' into a badge of honour. The former believed that war had a main cause (in their view, the Serbian leadership under Slobodan Mi-losevic) and that this was ascertainable through inquiry and thus had to be broadcast and written about in the name of objective journalism pursuing the truth.

The question of the BBC's position in journalism – not just in relation to other British media but also in relation to world media, where it is a large and important element – is critical. It is caught in a particular paradox. It is a state-funded broadcaster which must at the same time be independent in order to deserve its state-funded privileges. The modern British state would lose prestige if it had a slave broadcaster and no British parliament would support it. At the same time, its independence cannot be that of the British newspaper culture. That culture has, of course, a big influence on its editorial executives and reporters. But if the BBC becomes indistinguishable from the newspaper culture, it jeopardizes its privileges, since polemic in opinion columns and in reporting is being efficiently supplied by the market. It must thus find an independence which does not share the newspaper assumption that politicians are inherently objects of suspicion – a quest which, in the first years of the 2000s, it had in crucial parts of its output renounced.

That independence is to be found in a kind of journalism which Bell explicitly renounces. It is a journalism which assumes the existence of the truth and which has as its goal the finding of it. However, many journalists don't believe in the existence of truth – and certainly believe that, even if it does exist, it is unattainable by journalism. In an online debate organized in 2003, the discussion website Open Democracy canvassed a range of views from journal-ists, and observers of journalism, on how they should practise their craft. David Loyn, one of the BBC's foreign correspondents, argued that even if the goal of a 'single absolute truth' could never be reached, the effort must always be made. The view provoked some snorts of derision. In part, that tide was ridden by those who see the media as structurally biased – like Danny Schechter, editor of the US-based mediachannel.org, who called for a journalism which does 'more to examine how conflicts could be resolved rather than focus on the blood and the gore'. It is a line also taken by the journalist Jake Lynch, whose NGO Reporting the World seeks to popularize 'peace journalism', and who argues that 'journalists are always already involved, whether they like it or not'. Behind these arguments are the views of Pilger, Noam Chomsky and the film maker Michael Moore – who claim that either objectivity is impossible, or that the dominant media distort objective reality on behalf of various political or economic interests, or both. It was a rare voice in the debate which argued that objectivity is both desirable and at least theoretically possible; perhaps tellingly, the main representative of this view was not a media professional, nor a polemicist, but Julian Baggini, who is a philosopher.

Baggini chided Loyn for selling the pass too easily: if journalists' duty is to pursue truth, there must be a truth to pursue. He defines it as an increasingly objective perspective – the wider the frame of reference, the more transparent the process of selection and judgement in constructing the news, then the closer the reader or viewer can feel to an informed perspective.

The only broadcasting organization in Britain, and one of the few in the world, which has the resources and the tradition to attempt news whose objectivity is widely recognized, is the BBC. Although damaged by the kind of journalism of suspicion which was revealed by the Kelly affair, it retains the resources and the public and political support to develop the independence of informed view which is necessary to retain that support in the long term. With that goal in mind, Bell's 'journalism of attachment' must be a false trail.

In our interview, Bell had mentioned Fergal Keane, a fellow BBC reporter whose *Letter to Daniel*, a broadcast letter to his newly born son on the violence and poverty Keane had seen during his years in Africa (published in 1997) gave him a moral lustre which many listeners found attractive, though some found saccharine. Bell had commended it, but said it had encouraged bad imitations among BBC reporters of lesser talent. I called Keane, who had just done a long commentary on the Remembrance Sunday parade (9 November), and asked him about attachment journalism – expecting an endorsement. To my surprise, he vigorously rejected it – 'I don't believe reporters should be attached to anyone or anything' – and spoke from the position of one who was rethinking his journalistic attitudes.

> I'm weary of heart-on-the-sleeve journalism. I don't like the working assumption that all governments are wrong all the time. My experience in Northern Ireland and Africa showed me that the media tend to identify with an anti-government position, or with people they see as the underdogs. But look at Northern Ireland: actually, the people you had to understand there were the Ulster Protestants. Or the assumption made in South Africa that the ANC were always the good guys, when of course it's more complicated than that.

When I relayed to him Bell's view that he was widely and badly imitated, he said, 'I would hope not. I'm more and more aware of the limitations of journalism. You fly in and out of places and you make instant judgements because you must. The work I'm now most proud of are programmes which attempt to find out the facts and lay them out carefully.'

Keane, however, has been through a period of stardom achieved by public displays of emotion to achieve this view. The most prominent BBC reporter of 2003–4, Rageh Omaar, who reported from Baghdad throughout the invasion of Iraq, does seem to back the journalism of attachment. Indeed, he reproaches himself for not doing more editorializing:

> I did editorialize a bit. After all, I had been in and out of Iraq for seven years – and I used my pieces to camera before the war to say things about how ordinary Iraqis felt. But I didn't say there was a disaster coming. Maybe I should have said so. Maybe we all failed to say that there was a disaster coming after the war. There were a number of journalists who weren't there during the last years of Saddam, and who hadn't seen the country eviscerated by sanctions. We didn't point out how hard it would be after the war, because of what sanctions had done to Iraq. We should have said that before the war.

Omaar's book, *Revolution Day: the Human Story of the Battle for Iraq* (2004) stresses his engagement with ordinary people, and his ability to speak for them. In the Huw Wheldon lecture he gave to the Royal Television Society conference in September 2003 – an honour usually conferred on television's greybeards – he criticized the central position television coverage gave to the toppling of a statue of Saddam in central Baghdad as, 'an easy to comprehend image put on for the media to show the toppling of Saddam Hussein', and he suggested that 'the image of young doctors carrying guns to protect their patients' would 'speak more eloquently' on Iraq's future. Omaar is right to draw attention to the use of powerful, iconic images in television. But he is not against the use of powerful images which editionalize: he is calling for a different image conveying a different judgement. The hospital image says that things will get worse, while the statue-toppling image says that things can only get better. Yet who can know? Omaar cannot, for all his courage and expertise, yet he believes, with Bell, that a reporter on the spot is able to make these definite calls.

The view that journalism can never be objective and thus it must become 'attached' or 'engaged' or 'advocating' is now at the centre of controversy within the profession. Bell, as he pointed out to me, was made the subject of a polemical pamphlet – *Whose war is it anyway?* – put out by the magazine *Living Marxism* during the Bosnian conflict and written by its then editor and present *Times* columnist Mick Hume. Hume thought Bell was a bleeding heart – one who, with colleagues such as CNN's Christiane Amanpour, Newsday's Roy Gutman and the *Guardian*'s Ed Vulliamy, had turned suffering Bosnians into 'cannon fodder for their personal crusades'. *Living Marxism* agreed, objectively as Marxists say, with Douglas Hurd, on a dislike of the 'something must be done brigade'; others, such as Pilger and Chomsky, went still further, seeing in the journalism an endorsement of US imperialism's desire to squash socialist Serbia.

Ironically, Britain's most famous war reporter no longer wishes to engage in the conflict; for him, there are certain verities and they are largely dismal. The world has grown not honest, but dishonest and shallow, peopled by elegantly coiffed young men and women who describe wars they do not see to an audience which does not care, like the anonymous reporter on the 1991 Gulf war whom he mentions in *Through Gates of Fire*: 'a young and good-looking Canadian who apparently had a following among the ladies and who reported for the American network NBC on some explosive development in the war during the half-time break in the Super-bowl'. Much of what he says is conventional cynicism, about both politics and journalism, including the breathtaking remark, in his book, that 'the great American tradition of telling truth to power was incinerated in New York on 11 September 2001' – an observation that the most casual reading of any decent US news-

181

paper or magazine, or viewing or listening to any one of dozens of
news or discussion shows on TV or radio, would itself incinerate.

The practise of a journalism of attachment – that journalists bear
passionate witness, that experience brings the right to editorialize –
is one worth having. Television, and especially the BBC, has a
proud record of a journalism of attachment: programmes, whether
fictional or reality-based, which drew attention to scandals and
horrors, and implicitly or explicitly call for action. But these are not
news programmes. It is when Bell or Omaar or others (especially
others with less talent and courage) call for 'something to be done'
on mainstream news programmes that the problems begin. Policy
prescriptions have to come properly labelled – or broadcasters take
over the roles of elected politicians and displace them. The BBC has
sold that pass: indeed, it seems not to recognize the problem.

The best testimony on this I know is by the writer Michael
Ignatieff, who himself made TV documentaries and reported on the
wars of a disintegrating Yugoslavia. In a 1998 essay, he makes the
point that 'whether it wishes it or not, television has become
the principal mediation between the sufferings of strangers and
the consciences of those in the world's few remaining zones of
safety . . . it has become not merely the means through which we
see each other, but the means by which we shoulder each other's
fate.' Ignatieff makes a similar point to Little – that moral disgust
has its limits. But he goes further, suggesting that moral disgust can
become the antithesis of what Bell aims for: that is, it can turn into
sour indifference.

> As a moral mediator between violent men and the audiences whose
> attention they crave, television images are more effective at pre-
> senting consequences than in exploring intentions, more adept
> at pointing at corpses than in explaining why violence may, in
> certain places, pay so well. As a result television news bears some

182

responsibility for that generalized misanthropy, that irritable resignation towards the criminal folly of fanatics and assassins, which
legitimizes one of the dangerous cultural moods of the time – the
feeling that the world has become too crazy to deserve serious
reflection.

Deepening the Democratic Stake

NEWSPAPERS may be dying. It's now a possibility raised in many countries: in Sweden, the first to introduce a free sheet which sought readers like a newspaper; in France, where the newspaper culture tends to the elitist; even in Britain, where newspapers are more numerous than any other wealthy country, and very widely read. In an elliptical comment in March 2004, Alan Rusbridger, editor of the *Guardian* – who had seen his paper's circulation tumble by 30–40,000 in a year, apparently because of the decision of the *Independent* and *The Times* to go tabloid and thus win new sales – said that his 'truly radical stroke' was to create the most popular website of any newspaper, thus putting the *Guardian* in 'pole position on the web'. He continued: 'You know, there is an argument that all this debate about newspaper sizes is just deckchairs on the *Titanic*, compared to that'. Rusbridger, whose diagrammatic representation of what's happening to newspapers under siege from the Internet (see page 75) made everyone at a high-level media conference sit up and listen, clearly has an open mind about whether or not he will be the last editor of Britain's liberal newspaper – at least in the form in which he took it over.

There *is* such an argument as Rusbridger describes. And with it goes the fear that, in a no doubt slow death of newspaper culture, what will die with it is a part of democratic life. If, as Gunnar

Stromblad fears, the space for argument, dissent and inconvenient news is reduced because of the free sheets and the Internet, then there is no guarantee that anything will take its place. Newspapers which do difficult news are themselves difficult to found, to sustain and to develop. If advertising bases drop (they are low as this is written) and circulation drops with them, then they will cut pricey news in favour of cheaper polemic. They are already doing so.

The generation which would have had its views of public life formed more by newspapers than television are at least in their forties now – more often, fifties and above. Those who are the children of the TV age are not yet the majority in the leadership generations: but they will be soon. Newspapers have turned every which way to try to retain sales: now, they are turning to the Internet, in the hope that – if it comes to it – they can transfer their editorial output and tradition from paper to screen.

That may be fine for societies. Susanna Popova (p. 73) may be right – that democracy doesn't need a special room. And that the web is more democratic because much more information on it is more accessible – and everyone can be his or her own reporter, columnist and editor – as well as call on a much larger array of both news and opinion than that available in any newspaper.

'Newspapers' may become screen-based centres, branded as The *Guardian* or The *Sun*, for entering into vast stores of information accessible by individuals at times of their choosing – rather than a menu fixed for a day of what an editorial team considers important. But the move is likely to leave a gap, at least as large as it is today, where a broad-based, public service provision of explanation about the world should be. The argument that the media should do better at fulfilling the high responsibility they claim – to be guarantors of democratic, civil societies – will probably not be diminished in force. It will have to be put within the press – however that develops. Above all, it will have to be argued in

TV, which seems likely to continue to be the dominant medium, including the dominant medium for news, for many years. In the press, where controls are minimal (though would that continue if it became screen-based?) and government should have little standing as a regulator, the argument for content which informs society has to be made by concerned journalists. In television, the argument is inevitably one which involves governments and politics. The argument, as we've seen, increasingly lies between those who see little or no role for regulation on content and those who do. The arguments which form the conclusion of this essay fall into the latter camp; but many of them are not just arguments about public broadcasters, but about the media as a whole.

The questioning of public figures has to draw out discussion by treating politics and public life in general as an area where rational inquiry can illuminate difficult issues. The present habit of emphasizing and concentrating on the neuralgic issues – of splits, personal setbacks and insufficiencies, humiliations, betrayals of pledges – weaves a view of the public sphere as a hag-ridden crisis. Rational and courteous inquiry is the example the media should set, and insist on for their interviewees. That is, public figures should feel obliged to talk through their projects and proposals in depth and with evidence.

This approach is the opposite of complaisant journalism – the charge usually levelled at it. It insists on seriousness and is designed to expose its lack. Its object is understanding, and its procedure is to show what views, policies and constraints construct the actions of the public figure and to highlight the insufficiencies of these. It needs time for the interview itself; and the approach will also need time to establish its right to attention and to respect, both of the audience and on the part of those who submit themselves to its questioning. It requires a lot of experience and strength on the part

187

of the interviewer, as well as deep briefing on the issues; and it needs to be produced and promoted in a way which speaks to its seriousness and purpose – that of an all-out effort to understand the central issues of policy, politics, corporate life and public affairs, most of which have little such interrogation. If the aim is to illuminate our public life rather than to degrade it, or express contempt for those who practise it, then the act of interrogating politicians, public officials, corporate managers and others who play a public role – the interview – has to be rethought for its enlightenment, rather than for its calorific values.

One could mae an analogy with the Slow Food movement in Italy – a movement which emphasises that time is needed to prepare, serve and eat good food properly. Time is needed to prepare, publish and understand careful journalism which explains the workings of society to its citizens. Now might be a good time to start a 'slow journalism' movement.

Especially in the UK, a climate has grown around the coverage of and debate on politics which produces fear and tension – on both sides. It produces, not revelations, but silence, or pre-rehearsed blandness. Estelle Morris, the former British education secretary who resigned in 2003 because – among other reasons – she could not bear media pressure and intrusion, said in a later interview that 'we live at a time when [senior] politicians and celebrity are one and the same. I needed more privacy than I found myself able to get. Society has to ask itself: does it want to have politicians who act like they must when they're under the media spotlight? Politicians would like to be more frank, more honest – but they can't – because then they're slaughtered by the media.'

Debate on the media may never lead us to the truth: but it allows us to evaluate positions, policies and characters. It, too, needs time and space: but it also needs rules which are often the opposite of those in force now. Rather than stir up controversy – which usually means yelling, interruption and exaggeration – the aim would be to make clear the differences, and see where they really, as against artificially, lie. The moderator of the debate is critical: she or he has to constantly force the participants back to real issues, rather than point scoring; and thus the debate must be constructed so that this happens. That needs more than firmness on the part of the moderator and goodwill on the part of those who take part (though it does need these). It needs the use of studio techniques to illuminate their positions as they develop; it needs the use of the Internet to lay out previously taken positions; and it needs some kind of evaluative process after the debate to give a sense of how it's going. Like the interview, debate of this kind assumes complexity and difficulty; it doesn't take the implicit view, now the common one underlying much current affairs output, that understanding comes through exposure of a personal or a political weak point (it may be part of it).

Transparency has to be a principle of news coverage – which means that news coverage has to work consciously against the distortions to which the medium and its environment makes it prey. Competition distorts it: it strives to be more dramatic than the next news. Time distorts it: it has to turn round new little nuggets of news in a few hours. Twenty-four-hour news distorts it: reporters have to go on air with tiny amounts of knowledge about vast subjects. The sheer weight of event after horror after crisis after celebrity which is the modern news bulletin distorts: what picture of the world are we left with? Michael Ignatieff writes that:

> in the mingling of heterogeneous news stories, and in the enforcement of the regime of time, the news makes it impossible to attend to what one has seen. In the end one only sees the news, its person-

189

alities, its rules of selection and suppression, its authoritative voice. In the end, the subject of the news is the news itself . . . in this worship of itself, of its speed, its immense news gathering resources, its capacity to beat the clock, the news turns all reality into 90 second exercises in its own style of representation.

If that description implies that there is nothing to be done about this, however, it's probably too pessimistic. When news is short and telegraphic, it must also be transparent about its brevity and insufficiency. TV news bulletins have the edge in this: technology allows the screen to be split, so that the brief announcement can be supplemented with references to more information and other views. That is, it announces in its form that the main bulletin is the best version *at* the time and *within* the time, but that other versions exist. As with newspapers, television needs to refer to a much wider network of news (and analysis, context and opinions) than it can give. If it is to break out of the solipsistic iron circle which Ignatieff describes, then it must cease the pretence that (as CBS' most famous newsreader, Walter Cronkite, used to say at the end of his broadcast) 'that's the way it is'; and it must accept, and encourage, the fact that its audience, or part of it, wishes to interrogate the preconceptions of the news itself. One way of encouraging such engagement is to make clear the sources of the news and the alternative analyses from both official and unofficial sources. To provide a summary, and to encourage those who wish to, to be their own news editors.

The same applies to current affairs programmes. The narrative line taken in a documentary is always only one of several. Rageh Omaar's example (see page 180) of preferring an image of chaos to one of triumph in the overthrow of the Ba'ath regime in Iraq is an illumination of the issue which constantly and inevitably confronts television news-makers: in what frame do we construct our version of reality? Journalists and news producers must, of course, choose one. Even where that is done with respect to the conflicting and contradictory facts which usually attend any event, and pay some attention to the context in which these facts fit, they and we are left with a version which is open to endless revision. We should be allowed to submit it to some of that revision: it would clarify that what we are being offered is only a version of events and make us more active in considering alternatives.

Complicity between journalists and their subjects is usually there in some form. The best that can be done – and it is a good best, when well done – is to make such complicity transparent. The only way to do that is to show the mechanisms of the story when doing the story. The readers and audience have to be given clear pointers as to the reliability of the facts presented as such: even more importantly, to their possible unreliability, if no reliable ones are available. Insofar as the journalist gets engaged in the story, she or he has to make clear the engagement. An 'engaged' piece of journalism can be just as insightful as a detached one, as long as it's not the first masquerading as the second, and as long as it acknowledges it's not telling other sides of the story (if it isn't).

A search for objectivity and truth may seem like a contradiction to this: if news embraces transparency to admit that there are many versions of the truth, then why search for something so elusive? It's worth pursuing, though, because the search for an objective truth on which reasonable people can agree is the truth is assumed in the workings of our world. Laws, justice and government itself are all constructed on an implicit belief in objective truth: if journalism were to abandon the search, it would put itself at odds with the world it attempts to describe – and this it's in no position to do. Free, inquiring journalism depends utterly on the existence of a law-governed, rationally conducted public sphere. Once it assumes,

191

tacitly or openly, that all versions of reality within that sphere are equally valid, then it will sooner or later lose its moorings.

Newspapers can do some of this, but in their freedom, they don't have to. Most of them tend, at least now in Britain, to polemicize the world, rather than seek an understanding of it. Only a public service broadcaster has both the opportunity and duty to understand it. In his report of 29 May 2003, Andrew Gilligan had the beginnings of what might have been a large truth. He had a thread which, if pulled skilfully, could have revealed much about the nature of decision making on the British preparations for war in Iraq. But he broke off – for essentially short-term, polemical reasons. He proposed a reality through an inaccurate account of the evidence of one semi-insider's belief of what might have happened. His quest for an aspect of the truth was right: but he came nowhere near the end of the road down which he had begun to travel. The facts he began to uncover were only ever comprehensible in the round: when as much as possible of the context could be explained, and the decisions taken, the pressures involved and the outcomes, planned and unplanned, could be laid out. That takes time to make and to watch or to read, but it acts as a kind of gold standard to which the public can refer: it can provide a floor of objectivity on which opinions and revelations can be placed and weighed.

Such journalism is the opposite of 'establishment' or 'pro-government' journalism. It takes on the responsibility of trying to tell a whole truth. It means taking the initiative, and gaining an independent understanding of the world. Among newspapers and broadcasting institutions, only a tiny number in the world can mobilize the large resources needed for this job.

Those news organizations which do have the resources and intellectual authority to search for an understanding of the world set their own agenda. It will at times agree with some of the views and priorities of the public authorities; at times come to differing conclusions; at times reveal what is inconvenient to them. If it does not set such an agenda – based on the evident search for as full as possible an understanding of the world – an organization like the BBC must always run scared, because it is not doing the job which citizens who pay for it have the right to expect. That is, having complexities explained: debates supported by information and analysis; and the problems, contradictions and disguises of public life made less opaque.

Balance in the media is, in its most obvious sense, relatively easily achieved. Journalists can measure column inches or broadcast minutes devoted to the views and policies of one party or the other: and where there is a duty to be balanced, such as broadcasters have, they can demonstrate fidelity to that duty. But balance is only the beginning. An understanding of politics doesn't just come from equal weight given to programmes and statements at election – or any other – time. It comes from an understanding not just of the policies, but of how policies become projects and pass into reality. It comes not just from a demonstration that there are differing politics – but from an understanding of what politics is capable of, what it does and how it does it.

Understanding politics, business, social issues, international affairs, demands specialist knowledge – the more (usually) the better. Journalists, who are generally generalists, could use a lot more specialist training than they get. Even in big newspapers and broadcasting institutions, training in and knowledge of the subject or region which the reporter is assigned to cover, and the editor assigned to edit, can be minimal. The cult of the generalist, the limits of which have long been widened in the civil service, remains in tight force in the media. It can lead to basic misconceptions in coverage.

But there is a more important consideration than specialist training. The best reporting, which has a chance of approaching the truth, is done with an astringent human sympathy. That is, it can discriminate between sympathy and sentimentality, and does not pretend to sympathy when it is in fact an obeisance to power – still and always a prime journalistic temptation. It is that journalism which takes as its task the illumination of its subject, from within as well as from the outside.

'From within' doesn't mean the private life; on the contrary, private life shouldn't be touched by journalism, except with the express volition of the person who wishes to explore his or her private life. Or in these rare occurrences – the British monarchy's doings is one – in which the private, usually sexual, arrangements actually have a bearing on public life. In the monarchy's case, their private life has to be an issue of public concern because one of the fruits of royalty's loins will become the British head of state. And thus the royal loins are a legitimate area of interest.

The reporter should try to enter into what she or he deduces is the 'inner public' life of those on whom she or he reports: that is, she or he seeks to understand what the choices might really be, and what life really is like for the person described. Orville Schell, once a *New Yorker* writer and now dean of the Journalism School at University of California at Berkeley says that the *New Yorker* training was to give the writer

a basic presumption that you'll find some fundamental empathy with your subject. You could be critical, but to write from a perspective of mockery, disdain or overblown cynicism is dangerous . . . the whole point was to try to find where you connected with your topic and cared about it. That's certainly not the predominant sentiment behind much of what gets written nowadays, which is very flip, even savage, and often contemptuous. This tends to create a climate where everybody, writers included, feel very vulnerable, very attacked and insecure.

194

We in Britain, more than in any other modern state, have developed a 'laser-guided' journalism. It is the opposite of the journalism Schell invokes; it is also the opposite of what good news journalism demands. Such news journalism demands that it describes issues, events and public figures in the round, with an understanding of the environment in which they work. Laser-guided journalism goes straight to what it conceives of as the heart of darkness and remains there, demanding an explanation for the darkness on its own terms. The relative weight of what is seen as the heart of darkness is not its business: by shining its laser-guided beam on it, it elevates it to an absolute importance. And since media are much lighter on their feet than democratically mediated power – which is rooted in institutions, legislation and office – they can pass on to the next heart of darkness while the first is still having palpitations.

Ian Hargreaves writes that 'journalists are not lone rangers with a pocketful of silver bullets; they are individuals operating within an understood economic, cultural and political framework.' Laser-guided journalism depends on a pervasive contempt for the governing classes, especially for politicians; a definition of all official or corporate public relations and briefings as 'spin'; a concentration on process at the expense – often to the complete obliteration – of policy and outcomes; a privileging of conflict and complaint and a dramatization of ordinary conflict, such as within government, as crises, irrespective of any tendency to contain the conflict with compromise.

This produces the opposite of what a journalism devoted to public understanding would wish to produce. We need to think how we would like the world to be represented to us in a way in which most of us – on a 'reasonable people' test – would agree was . . . reasonable. It's one of the most important things journalism can come up with, to save itself from the scorn which threatens to engulf it. And it will engulf it. In the 2002 Reith lectures, the philosopher Onora O'Neill gave over the last of her lectures, on the theme of 'trust', to the media. It was uncomfortable listening. The media, she said, were the only unregulated great power left – and that power was used, often, to abuse public trust. 'We are now perilously close,' she said, 'to a world in which media conglomerates act as if they . . . had unrestricted rights of free expression, and therefore a licence to subject positions for which they don't care to caricature and derision, misrepresentation or silence.'

The media, by what they're doing, fail to make us understand the world. And they fail to make us understand the world in a way which often lets governments, and every other public and private body, off the hook. If the media are always getting it wrong – indeed, claim the *right* to get it wrong, and don't seem to care when they do – then governments and other institutions don't need to be held to account by them. And that, in the end, is the worst outcome of all: media which allow debasement to so dilute the function which their ideals trumpet that they can no longer fulfil it, and societies become the worse for it. It is not the situation in which we find ourselves yet, but it could be; and it is one which we in the media have visited, and are visiting, on ourselves and then on everybody else.

Politicians and other public figures have to stop collaborating with the worst media practises: in fact, the media can't reform themselves without this. Above all, politicians must do what Estelle Morris said they are afraid of doing: insist on broadcasting space in which proper examination and debate takes place. This they can do in two ways: by making laws, and by example.

In framing the BBC Charter – as well as the conditions under which other broadcasters broadcast, and the criteria the new regulatory body for the communications industry, Ofcom, must apply – the aim must be to retain a framework which the US has progressively abandoned. That is, of providing what the market doesn't provide: the public good of good news, current affairs, debate and cultural coverage. It is on Ofcom – which started work at the beginning of 2004 – that the responsibility to define what public service journalism can be, has largely fallen.

How do you secure the ideal which James Fallows has outlined – 'the information necessary for democratic decisions'? What if the market doesn't allow it? The Ofcom official who had to think most about this is Ed Richards, a former BBC policy planner and adviser to Tony Blair on broadcasting, now one of two senior partners of Ofcom. Richards came at the job with a view which he called the 'social market' approach. That is, he thought that, even though technology and conventional wisdom was careening after the easy market solution and forgetting about what broadcasting owed the public, the attempt should be made to hold back the market tides. Yet, faced with a review of public service broadcasting to be completed in 2004 – a review which would feed directly into the discussions on the renewal of the BBC Charter, to be completed by 2006 – he was under few illusions about the limits to his power.

Ofcom – along with the government – could try to even the playing field as between the BBC and independent television, bringing the latter at least up to the level of the former in the provision of news and current affairs. But if the independent companies were faced with such demands, some of them (not Channel 4) might say to Richards: we'll relocate offshore – like the pirate radios of the 1950s and 1960s – or go digital once the coverage of households approaches the 90 per cent range. No one has any responsibilities in the digital sector – beyond the technical ones. There, they could do as they liked: and the 'public service' sector would be vacant, except for the BBC. If, through the European Union, common standards were set for all broadcasters, the shift on to the continent could be blocked off. But European standards differ hugely; getting agreement on how many hours of what quality of public service TV would be a long-drawn-out, and perhaps fruitless, process.

Richards was facing the same arguments which had been made – successfully – by Murdoch and many others in the US: indeed, *were* being made there by Michael Powell, the chairman of the US equivalent of Ofcom, the FCC. Powell believed, he said in an interview, that complaints about the lack of public service information were essentially ideological, and the government regulator shouldn't be concerned with such things. 'Either you don't see enough of something you like, or you see too much of something you don't. But at the end of the day, you have to ask whether you want . . . unelected regulators saying: I want the public to see this but not that.' Powell was appointed by a government of the right (he is the son of Secretary of State Colin Powell) and Richards by a government of the left, but they both face the same question, the one Powell posed.

The argument made constantly to Richards and his colleagues at Ofcom, was: if current affairs is shrinking on TV, does it really matter? The core of the public service is news and information. News, information, and analysis and commentary, is available in much larger amounts than it has ever been before – in the upmarket newspapers, in specialist publications and above all on the Internet. So what are we worrying about?

Richards could see the point of such an argument. He knew that many people – like him – took in huge draughts of information, usually in printed form, from newspapers, magazines, pamphlets, books and printed out from the Internet. Within a mile or so radius of his office on the south bank of the Thames, some forty or fifty think-tanks were hard at work, full of motivated youngish people like himself, publishing, arguing, advocating and lobbying – a huge growth in the past two decades. If you wanted to know a lot about the Chinese energy market, the Colombian terrorist problem or the state of the French left, you could assemble a weekend of steady reading in an hour or so. Why wait for the 'Panorama' programme or the 'Newsnight' spot to tell you? Why crowd out

'EastEnders' or 'The Simpsons' for something obtained in much greater detail, more efficiently, elsewhere?

The answer Richards came up with was not a comfortable one, given the trends in the mass media market. It is the opposite of the approach adopted by Michael Powell at the FCC: it is a re-assertion of the view that citizens need information, analysis and argument to enjoy their rights and fulfil their duties as citizens, and that TV must provide some of that for them. Indeed, it is the recognition that one part of the citizenry has the tools to be fabulously information-rich through the profusion of information available, which bolsters that argument. It recognizes that very many are information poor, and seeks to redress the balance. Richards also saw the whole notion of an 'objective' approach to news crumbling. The Kelly affair had been, he thought, an egregious example of the BBC giving up on proper objectivity, but there was more to the issue than that. More and more households were discovering the delight of having their own prejudices confirmed, rather than challenged. Fox News was now available: so was Al Jazeera, the pan-Arab channel (originally set up by the BBC).

The Reithian virtues had to be modernized, and restored. If this were to be done at the price of some intrusion – even, of being a bit of a nanny-knows-best – then so be it. To take this approach is to swim against a tide of trends and assumptions, some of which have been described above. But if that isn't done, then there is no alternative. If it isn't done, and the media don't 'rise' to the challenge of citizenship, then – as Pulitzer warned – the citizens could, over time, become debased.

The same challenge lies before the BBC. Its top leadership – chairman and director general – went almost immediately after the publication of the Hutton Report. It thus had the chance to do its own, new, thinking on what public service broadcasting might mean, in synchronization with Ofcom. The BBC has a reputation, unrivalled in the world, for accuracy, objectivity and authority. It can recover it: but it will take some doing.

Politicians can and did secure the Ofcom regulatory structure: politicians can and do debate and decide the terms of the BBC Charter. But they need to give an example, as well. I have tried to sketch how New Labour treated the media before and during government, and the pressures that made them do so. The approach they came up with was certainly proactive and aggressive at times, yet it also opened up areas to the media to which they had not previously had access. Innovations included making clear that advice came from a prime ministerial spokesman; and a monthly on-the-record press conference by the prime minister. Human rights legislation opened up information to scrutiny which had been closed.

But the approach had a large downside. It became – perhaps always was – manipulative. It included rewards and punishments; it depended on rewarding favourites who write or broadcast well; denigrating those who write or broadcast accurately, but inconveniently. It worked by playing media off against each other, telling, if not lies (which happened, but were and are rare) at least highly slanted versions of reality; acquiescing to an attitude of confrontation and cynicism without confronting it in turn.

Most leading politicians believe something like Estelle Morris: they certainly say so, loudly, usually off the record, occasionally on. But if the media are to improve, they need these complaints to be voiced; more, they need politicians to challenge them to report better, interview better, conduct debates better. Public figures need to point out to the media when they believe they are harming public life – on the media. Politicians have the power of representing the electorate: they must pit it directly against those who draw their power from a less solid base.

*   *   *

Democratic politics needs the assistance of the media: the power struggle between them reduces our public sphere. The challenge for the media, as John B. Thompson writes, is 'to find ways of deepening the democratic stake by enlarging the scope of the democratic process'. What could this mean?

I think it should mean making many programmes *with* rather than *against* those who carry on democratic and civic life. It would mean using the extraordinary presentational skills of contemporary television to deepen and enliven the democratic process. Parliaments and assemblies, political meetings and rallies, trades union conferences, companies' annual meetings, think-tanks, professional associations, senior citizens' groups, school and university debating societies, even editorial meetings, could all be made part of the media diet. There could be programmes which connect what happens in the parliamentary chamber or select committees or town halls with what happens in schools, offices or hospitals – which show how people deliberate, dispute and decide in their own time and in their own places about public matters. It would be a project worthy of the talent which flows into TV: an anti-Big Brother project, in both the Orwellian and Bazalgettian senses.

This is not, of course, how media see themselves. But it would mark a certain maturing, both of politics and of the media. Politics, at every level, would have to be prepared to be open to other media: it would be put on its mettle thereby. But the larger shift would come for the media: they would have to construct a wholly new approach to civic culture, which was not merely of treating it as a field in which they went hunting for stories, but also as one which should be directly reflected in their coverage – often without any mediation from journalists, or only with occasional neutral explanation. The task would be to make the central debating chambers which address and which legislate for our public life and our national interests interesting to a mass audience. It's a tall order, against stiff competition. But it would seem to be necessary for our civic health.

Michael Schudson observes of the US media that 'if journalists begin to ask seriously the question . . . what can the media do to improve the American democratic process – assuming an intelligent and interested electorate – they will find ways . . .' Some ways have already been found – the UK parliament, like many others, already has its own channel, and there is edited parliamentary debate on radio for 30 minutes every day when parliament is sitting. But many others exist to be found. The major speeches made by public figures could be presented in a setting which explains their background and analyses their main proposals and possible, or actual, effects: it would encourage better rhetoric. The main committees of parliament could be framed in a way which made their investigations compelling. The main exchanges in the Commons chamber, when sitting, could be a feature of daily news coverage. More ambitiously still – the deliberations of foreign legislatures should be part of our media fare: so we can better understand cultures which are often represented to us through crises, stereotypes, or the warm glow of televised tourism.

The aim would be clear: to attempt to re-establish representative democratic gatherings at the centre of public life. One of the media's major tropes has been the drop in support for politics and politicians; and, as we know from recent research by Robert Putnam, one of the causes of the public indifference to politics and lack of an engagement in civic life has been entertainment TV. The media cannot remain indifferent to a trend which is in part their doing; a public broadcaster has a duty to counteract a trend which so narrows the public space.

Media cannot, as its leading figures like to claim, substitute in any major way for the political struggle. It is not their job – for any presumed reason, such as weakness of the non-governing parties, lack of attendance at political meetings, drop in interest in parliament – to take upon themselves the business of being a political opposition. News media hold public figures to account, but the first line of doing so, and much the more important, is politicians of the opposition party who claim to be able to form a government themselves. Media have the right – the necessity, in a democracy – to maintain diversity, openness, to investigate, to attempt balance and objectivity. They have not the responsibility for opposing.

Representative democracy and discursive politics are everywhere under pressure. Most media, and many new political movements, implicitly or explicitly prefer some sort of plebiscite – through polls, or mass rallies, or audience figures – to the voting of representatives. It is clear from twentieth-century history to what dangers that leads. The strength of the British state, as of many others, has long been the ability of elected representatives to make the judgements and effect the compromises necessary to relatively peaceful, relatively prosperous, relatively equable and civilized life. The media have been the beneficiaries of that: time, now, to take a more active hand in its protection.

Can we imagine a journalism which is civic? One which defies its own natural instincts – to make celebrities of itself; which acts as an adjunct to activity and reflection; which presents to its audience first drafts of history which are absorbing and subtle, strong on narrative but attentive to the complexity and context of every story; which is not struggling with political power, but struggling, together with that power's best instincts, to make the contemporary world at once comprehensible and open to the participation of its citizens. If we can imagine it, we should be able to create it.

Postscript

The quotations below are from a talk with a senior member of the present (2004) Cabinet. Though drawn from one talk, it conforms closely to what I have found to be a consensual view within the Government, and among Government aides, civil servants and many opposition politicians. It is a view of the media as a largely undifferentiated, hostile mass. Or – to change metaphors – a capricious and cruel deity, which must be placated because of its power, but which will strike at whomever it wishes, whenever it wishes.

I don't think that the Mandy Rice Davies defence – 'they would say that, wouldn't they?' – is sufficient to dismiss these views. Even if these views were a delusion – that the media were, unnoticed by the political class, doing a proper and irreproachable job in preserving democratic values by providing citizens with the information and debate required to sustain an open and liberal polity – the possession of them by a large part of the political class would be a serious matter. It would mean that a huge gulf of misunderstanding had opened up between two great powers. It would be reasonable to suppose that society would, in the long run, be damaged by this.

The quotations are off the record, and are slightly altered to conceal the present post of the speaker. However, they are not distorted. It is a regret that most of what politicians and other public figures say about the media is off the record – first, because they cannot properly and openly be challenged; second and most importantly, because they cannot then lead a necessary debate on the nature of the media's representation of our society. Yet their rejoinder – that to do so would open them to further attack for no gain – is not easy to dismiss.

'The press is immensely competitive – and the media generally, much more than ever before. And they are not held to account. The one great thing that the Hutton Inquiry did was to hold them to account. For once someone went over the issue and held it up to the light.

'As a result of this competition, I don't feel the media report the news. They only report the news through a prism of sensation, scandal and confrontation. The news as such is not sufficiently interesting. I don't think there is much difference between the tabloids and the broadcasters. That's been the biggest change in the media in the last decade.

'The political journalists have more interest in becoming personal-ities than in putting across the news. They are anxious to give themselves as much importance as those who make the news.

'The aftermath of the Hutton Inquiry was as important as the story. Even I was surprised at the way in which the media transformed Lord Hutton, who was pretty irreproachable, into a government stooge within 48 hours. The build-up to Hutton was very important because the evidence was so distorted. For example the two Ministry of Defence people who raised questions about the 45-minute claim – had these been incorporated it wouldn't have made any difference to the dossier (on Iraq) put out.

'It's now commonplace that the attacks on politicians are personal because policy isn't seen as important enough. Yet the odd thing is, that in this government we've been more open than any government before us:

- We published intelligence about Iraq: never been done before.
- We had a vote on it [Iraq] in the House of Commons: never been done before.
- After the allegation by Andrew Gilligan, members of the Government appeared before the Foreign Affairs Committee for the first time.
- The Prime Minister appeared before the Security Committee: the first time a PM had done so. Indeed, I don't think a PM has ever appeared before any select committee before to give evidence.
- The Prime Minister appeared before the Hutton Inquiry to give evidence.

'I think it is true that we ran too much with the media agenda in opposition. I think there is something in saying that we were too complicit with the media. The issue of sleaze (in the Major Government) was a big public issue and sometimes you had to raise it. But it was a media tactic which could of course be used against us, and which was distasteful in some ways.

'The idea of holding the media to account is a crucial one. In every "scandal" in which the Government has been involved, most of what was written and broadcast was wrong and no one held any of the people who wrote these things to account, or subjected the things to scrutiny. In all of these, the reporters took a few grains of the truth and built a mountain of distortion. It's the distortion which is so bad.

'You have to ask the question: is it the purpose of the news media to make an impact or to report the news? It seems to be purely the impact. I cannot imagine what happens within a newspaper when a reporter writes a story which may or may not be true – does the

207

editor hold him to account? They seem to have little regard for the truth of the story.

'I've taken to looking over my speeches very carefully before they go out. If you use a particular word – and this has happened several times – the reporters will grab at it and twist it. I have to make sure there is absolutely nothing that can be misinterpreted. It's a curious situation: the journalists know you don't mean what they say you mean: you know it; yet the distortion is put across. The lobby briefings, for example, have become an elaborate game of "gotcha".

'I don't see much difference between the different papers. The *Financial Times*, *The Times* and *The Daily Telegraph* to an extent try to get it right. But even they are caught in the same traps.

'I think in retrospect it was wrong that the BBC was led by two New Labour supporters in Gavyn Davies and Greg Dyke. I felt at the time they were appointed, that the problem of loyalty would arise, and that they would feel they had to overcompensate for their New Labour credentials. They interpreted independence as a position in which they couldn't even examine their actions.

'The key thing is holding to account. The politicians are held to account – by Parliament, the opposition and by the media day-by-day; by the public in election and re-election. It's up to the media to hold itself to account: there's nothing much we can do in a democratic state.

'Other leading politicians elsewhere know the British media are different. They all say so. Especially the Americans, but also the Europeans. They say "our media is bad, but I wouldn't have yours for anything". The Press Complaints Commission is hopeless. Our media are very powerful – you could say they are the most powerful in the world. The US media are powerful but they're regional. Here we have an absolute concentration at the centre of a highly competitive media which doesn't have any cognate elsewhere.

'Maybe you could say we tried too hard to woo over the magnates – but if you make that critique you have to take into account the power of the media here. You must deal with it. If all the papers turned against the Government or the Prime Minister – more have now than before – it and he, could in the end be destabilized to the point of losing. It could happen. Look at Neil Kinnock. Neil said – to hell with them: I hate them and won't talk to them. And looked what happened to him.

'The *Daily Mail* is an extraordinary product. It springs from the head of Paul Dacre [the editor] who has the kind of prejudices and beliefs no one knows about. I won't go into them. But he is accountable to no one. He has absolute and unaccountable power.

'The BBC has been damaged by the Kelly affair. You can't say it's all bad because there are some very good bits to it. But it's no longer got the reputation it had.

'Look at the difference between Andrew Gilligan and Susan Watts. Gilligan sexed it up and Susan Watts by and large didn't. But look who got the space and the fame. No one had heard of her. He made the impact. These are the values – of the BBC and all the rest.

'All of this *does* matter. This is the way people are informed, and know what's going on in the world, and what's being done, supposedly in their name.'

Sources

Introduction

Colombani, Jean-Marie, 'Trois Défis', *Le Monde, Courrier International*, 'Le Tour du Monde en 80 Journaux', p. II.

Goldberg, Bernard, *Bias*, (Regnery, New York, 2002).

Graham, Katharine, *Personal History*, (Vintage, London, 1998), p. 508.

Marquand, David, *Decline of the Public*, (Polity Press, Cambridge, 2004), p. 2.

'Panorama', 21 January 2004.

Phillips, Melanie, 'America's Social Revolution', Civitas in association with the *Sunday Times*, 2001, p. 71.

Putnam, Robert, *Bowling Alone: The Collapse and Revival of American Community*, (Simon and Schuster, New York, 2002).

Schudson, Michael, *The Power of News*, (Harvard University Press, Cambridge, Massachusetts, 1995) p. 171.

Stephens, Philip, 'Blair is as determined as ever to achieve his goals', *Financial Times*, 30 January 2004, p. 21.

Young, Hugo, *Supping with the Devils: Political Journalism*, (Atlantic Books, New York, 2003), pp. xv–xvi.

As Free as the Society

Amadori, Alessandro, *Mi Consenta: Metafore, Messaggi e Simboli. Come Silvio Berlusconi Ha Conquistato il Consenso degli Italiani*, (Libri Schweiwiller, Milano, 2002), p. 159.

Annunziata, Lucia, *NO: la Seconda Guerra Irachena e I Dubbi dell'Occidente*, (Donzelli, Rome, 2002).

Bourdieu, Pierre, *On Television and Journalism* (Pluto Press, London, 1998), p. 48.

Ferenczi, Thomas, talk to the Centre for the Study of Democracy in London, October 2000. The quotes are from Pierre Bourdieu, *On Television*.

Frontori, Laura, *Il Mercato dei Segni,* (Cortina, Milano, 1988), quoted in *Mi Consenta,* p. 156.

Ginsborg, Paul, *Italy and its Discontents*, (Allen Lane: The Penguin Press, London, 2001), p. 290.

Hargreaves, Ian, *Journalism Truth or Dare*, (Oxford University Press, Oxford, 2003), p. 57.

Jones, Tobias, *The Dark Heart of Italy*, (Faber, London, 2003), p. 127.

Le Monde, 5 December 2003.

Le Monde, 12 and 13 February 2004.

Ovrebo, Olav Anders, 'When the Audience Becomes the Medium', *Axess Magazine*, Stockholm, No. 6, 2003.

Stead, W. T., 'The Future of Journalism', *Contemporary Review*, 1886; quoted in Ian Hargreaves, op. cit., pp. 49–50.

Tett, Gillian, 'Hogging the Script or Reading Between the Lines?' Speech to Unesco conference on the media, Tokyo, 2003.

The *New York Review of Books*, 23 May and 15 August 2003.

They Will Gobble You Up

Adie, Kate, *The Kindness of Strangers: the Autobiography*, (Headline Books, London, 2003), p. 355.

Asuletta, Ken, 'Fortress Bush', *New Yorker*, 19 January 2004.

Auletta, Ken, 'Vox Fox', *New Yorker*, 29 May 2003, p. 61.

Birt, John, *The Harder Path*, (Time Warner, London, 2002), pp. 255–6.

Blick, Andrew, *People Who Live in the Dark* (Politicos, London, 2004), pp. 251–96.

Fallows, James, *Breaking the News*, (Vintage, New York, 1996), p. 63.

Fallows, James, 'The Age of Murdoch', *Atlantic Monthly*, September 2003, p. 81.

Follett, Ken, *Observer*, 2 July 2000.

Giddens, Anthony, *Beyond Left and Right*, (Polity Press, Cambridge, 1994), pp. 49–50.

Goodhart, David, 'Who Are the Masters Now?, *Prospect*, May 1997, pp. 22–25.

Gopnik, Adam, 'Read all About It', *New Yorker*, 1994, pp. 84–102.

Gould, Philip, *The Unfinished Revolution: How Modernisation saved the Labour Party*, (Little, Brown, London, 1998), p. 170.

Humphrys, John, *The Devil's Advocate*, (Arrow Books, London, 2000), p. 224.

Ingham, Bernard, *The Wages of Spin* (John Murray, London, 2003).

Jamieson, Kathleen Hall and Waldman, Paul, *The Press Effect*, (Oxford University Press, New York, 2003), pp. 166–7.

Jones, Nicholas, *Campaign 1997* (Gollancz, London, 1997), p. 75.

Jones, Nicholas, *Campaign 2001: an Election Diary* (Politicos, London, 2001).

Jones, Nicholas, *Sultans of Spin* (Weidenfeld and Nicolson, London, 1999).

Jones, Nicholas, *The Control Freaks – How New Labour Gets its Own Way* (Politicos, London, 2002).

Kettle, Martin, 'The Threat to the Media is Real. It Comes From Within', *Guardian*, 3 February 2004.

Lambert, Richard, *Prospect*, March 2002.

MacFarquar, Larissa, 'The Populist', *New Yorker*, 16/23 February 2004, pp. 132–45.

McElwee, Martin and Gaskarth, Glyn, *The Guardian of the Airwaves?: Bias and the BBC*, (Cchange, London, 2003).

Oborne, Peter & Campbell, Alastair, *New Labour and the Rise of the Media Class*, (Aurum, London, 1999).

Pattersson, Thomas, *Out of Order*, (Knopf, New York, 1993).

Paxman, Jeremy, *The Political Animal: An Anatomy*, (Michael Joseph, London, 2002), p. 162.

Simpson, John, *A Mad Mad World, My Masters*, (Pan, London, 2001), p. 267.

Tannen, Deborah, *The Argument Culture*, (Ballantine, New York, 1998), pp. 58 and 77.

Wyatt, Will, *The Fun Factory: a Life In the BBC*, (Aurum Press, London, 2003), p. 307.

Greater Than Any of Them

Bell, Martin, *Through Gates of Fire*, (Weidenfeld and Nicolson, London, 2003.)

Blankley, Tony, 'Rush's Show Goes On', *Washington Times*, 10 October 2001.

Crossman, Fletcher, 'BBC vs Fox News: Fair and Balanced to you, too', *International Herald Tribune*, 10 February 2004, p. 6.

Ferenczi, Thomas, 'L'Ethique des journalistes au XIXe Siècle', in *Le Temps des Medias*, Autumn 2003, pp. 190–9.

Feyel, Gilles, 'Aux Origins de l'ethique des journalistes', in *Le Temps des Medias*, Nouveau Monde, No. 1, Autumn 2003.

Financial Times Magazine, 1 November, 2003, p. 7.

Humphrys, John, 'Journalists getting it badly wrong can be good for you', *Sunday Times*, 8 February 2004, p. 19.

Ignatieff, Michael, 'Is nothing sacred: the ethics of television', in *The Warriors' Honour*, (Vintage, London, 1999), pp. 24–5.

Massing, Michael, 'Now they tell us', *New York Review of Books*, 26 February 2004, pp. 43–9.

Maupassant, Guy de, *Bel Ami*, (Penguin Books, London, 1975), p. 96.

Mill, J.S., *On Liberty*, (Penguin, London, 1974).

Sampson, Anthony, *Who Runs This Place?*, (John Murray, London, 2004), p. 207.

Schudson, Michael, 'Question Authority: a history of the news interview' in *The Power of News*, (Harvard University Press, Cambridge, Massachusetts, 1995.)

Smith, Anthony, *The Newspaper: an International History*, (Thames and Hudson, London, 1979), p. 30.

Trollope, Anthony, *The Warden*, (JM Dent Everyman Library edition, London, 1975.)

Yergin, Daniel, *The Prize*, (Simon and Schuster, New York, 1992), pp. 100–109.

Zakaria, Fareed, in a conversation with the author in April 2003.

Zengerle, Jason, 'Talking Back', *The New Republic*, 16 February 2004, pp. 172.

Deepening the Democratic Stake

Grande, Carlos, 'How will the Guardian measure up to the contacts?' *FT Creative Business*, 16 March 2004.

Hargreaves, Ian, *Journalism Turth or Dare*, (Oxford University Press, Oxford, 2003), p. 17.

Ignatieff, Michael, *The Warrior's Honour*, (Vintage, London, 1999), p. 30.

O'Neill, Dr Onora, Reith Lectures, 2002, BBC Radio 4.

Putnam, Robert, *Bowling Alone*, (Simon and Schuster, New York, 2002).

Tannen, Deborah, *The Argument Culture* (Ballantine, New York, 1998), p. 91.

Thompson, John B., *Media and Modernity*, (Polity, Cambridge, 1995), p. 257.

Walden, Brian, interview with Estelle Morris, BBC Radio 4, 22 February 2004.

Index